一粒小米的故事

The story of a millet

主编	王慧军	Wang Huijun
Editors in Chief	张韶斌	Zhang Shaobin

 中国大地出版社

·北　京·

委员
Committee Members

柴 岩	陈亚春	冯国郡
Chai Yan	Chen Yachun	Feng Guojun
高爱农	管延安	郭二虎
Gao Ainong	Guan Yan'an	Guo Erhu
郭平毅	何红中	李保安
Guo Pingyi	He Hongzhong	Li Bao'an
李海霞	李书田	刘 猛
Li Haixia	Li Shutian	Liu Meng
刘文周	马天进	裴 莉
Liu Wenzhou	Ma Tianjin	Pei Li
任庆帅	谭天章	田秀娟
Ren Qingshuai	Tan Tianzhang	Tian Xiujuan
杨 平	杨天育	袁宏安
Yang Ping	Yang Tianyu	Yuan Hong'an
张 云	张喜文	郑建英
Zhang Yun	Zhang Xiwen	Zheng Jianying
周 潇		
Zhou Xiao		

张瑞奇
Zhang Ruiqi

英文翻译
English Translators

刘妮雅　　　李晓芝　　　周语潮
Liu Niya　　Li Xiaozhi　　Zhou Yuchao

刘国庆　　　曹建如　　　吴　哲
Liu Guoqing　Cao Jianru　　Wu Zhe

程　璐
Cheng Lu

艺术顾问
Artistic Advisers

陈九元　　　陈国强
Chen Jiuyuan　Chen Guoqiang

设计
Designers

魏　敏　　　陈小冬
Wei Min　　Chen Xiaodong

王慧军

Wang Huijun

王慧军，男，1957年3月出生，汉族，1975年1月参加工作，二级教授，河北农业大学、东北农业大学博士生导师。河北省高端人才，资深优秀省管专家，享受国务院特殊津贴。现任河北省杂粮实验室主任，曾任河北农业大学副校长、河北省农林科学院院长，为我国农业推广学学科创始人之一，出版著作20余部，发表学术论文100余篇，获国家及省部级科技奖励10余项。

一粒小米的故事
The story of a millet

主编简介

Introduction of Editors in Chief

Professor Wang Huijun, born in March 1957, started his career in January 1975, is a distinguished professor of Hebei Agricultural University and Northeast Agricultural University. He is the current Director of Minor Cereal Crops Research Laboratory of Hebei Province at present. He is a high-end talent and outstanding expert in Hebei, and enjoys the Government Special Allowance by the State Council. Prof. Wang was the Vice President of Hebei Agricultural University and President of Hebei Academy of Agriculture and Forestry Sciences. He is one of the co-founders of agricultural extension and has published more than 20 books and 100 papers. He was awarded over 10 national and provincial and ministerial level awards in science and technology .

张韶斌
Zhang Shaobin

张韶斌，男，1970年9月出生，1994年7月参加工作，河北省农业广播电视学校校长。曾任河北省农垦局副局长、河北省农业农村厅人事处副处长等职。曾主持"省农村青年拔尖人才强化培训""省农村实用人才带头人能力提升""全省乡村振兴人才队伍建设专题研究""产业＋人才融合发展模式剖析"等"人才强冀"工程。

一粒小米的故事
The story of a millet

Mr. Zhang Shaobin, born in September 1970, started work in July 1994, is the Headmaster of Hebei Agricultural Radio and Television School. He used to be the Deputy Director of Hebei Bureau of Agricultural Reclamation and the Deputy Director of Human Resources Division of Hebei Agriculture and Rural Affairs Department. He has presided over such projects as "the intensive training of top-notch talents for provincial rural youth" "On improving the ability of practical talents leaders in provincial rural areas" "Special research on the construction of talents for provincial rural revitalization" "Analysis on the integrated development mode of industry and talents" etc.

国家谷子高粱产业技术体系评审组意见

Review Comments from the Review Group of National Millet and Sorghum Industry Technology System

2019 年 1 月 4 日，国家谷子高粱产业技术体系组织专家组成评审组，在山西省太谷县对河北省农林科学院与河北正奇文化传播有限公司等单位创作的《粟说——一粒小米的故事》纪录片进行了评审。评审组听取了策划、编导人员的工作汇报，观看了纪录片，经认真讨论，形成如下意见：

On January 4th of 2019, the team of the National Millet and Sorghum Industry Technology System organizes the experts to form the review team to make evaluation, in Taigu County of Shanxi Province, on the documentary *The Story of a Millet* that is jointly produced by Hebei Academy of Agriculture and Forestry Sciences and Hebei Zhengqi Culture Communication Co. Ltd. The following remarks are given by the members of the review team after listening to the work report by the Planners and the Produce Directors, watching the documentary and discussing Carefully:

1. 该片从策划到播出，历时六年，跨越 13 个省（自治区、直辖市），行程 3 万多千米，走访了数十家科研单位、大专院校、企业，采访了上百名专家学者、企业家及农户，素材丰富、内容翔实、画面真实，内容体现了科学性、真实性，具有重要的史料价值。

1. The documentary has taken 6 years of production, from the planning to the broadcast. By crossing 13 provinces (autonomous region, municipality) and covering more than 30,000 km, the production team visited dozens of research institutes, universities, colleges and enterprises, interviewed hundreds of experts, entrepreneurs and farmers. This documentary has important historical value due to its wide coverage of geographical areas and subjects, diversified interviewees, rich and detailed materials, as well as the real pictures.

2. 该片首次以声像方式系统记录与表现了谷子这一中国起源作物的历史，展示了其在中华农耕文明形成中的地位与作用，为引导观众了解中华文明发展历史提供了丰富的声像资料。

2. The documentary systematically records and represents the history of foxtail millet, which is originated from China, firstly by the form of audio and video. It has important position and function in the formation of Chinese agricultural civilization, providing a wealth of audio-video information for leading the audience to understand the history of Chinese civilization development.

3. 该片由自然科学、社会科学人员共同策划与制作，深刻挖掘了谷子在中华民族优秀传统文化中所打下的物质、精神、文化、政治、科技、生态烙印，拓宽了谷子科学研究的视野。

3. The documentary is planned and produced by natural and social scientists jointly.

It has deeply explored the material, spiritual, cultural, political, scientific and technological, ecological imprints that millet laid on the excellent traditional culture of the Chinese nation, and broadened the perspective of millet research.

4. 该片普及了谷子种质资源学、遗传育种学、耕作栽培学、产品加工学及健康营养学等知识，为谷子产业发展、健康中国建设、和谐社会构建传播了科学知识，对谷子产业布局、产业链延伸、创新方向确定具有一定的指导意义。

4. The documentary has popularized the knowledge of foxtail millet's germplasm resources, genetics and breeding, tillage and culture, processing and health nutrition, spread scientific knowledge to promote millet industry development, healthy China construction and harmonious society construction. It has guiding significance for millet industrial distribution, extension of industrial chain and innovative direction.

5. 该片归纳了谷子具有逆境抗争、环境友好、生态和谐、谦逊报恩、健康营养等特征，体现了中华民族所蕴含的不屈不挠、和谐共生、天人合一的精神灵魂，符合新时代文化传播要求。

5. The documentary has summarized the millet's characteristics such as being resistant to stresses, friendly to environment, harmonious to ecology, modest and grateful, healthy and nutritious. It reflects the spirit of the Chinese nation of perseverance, inclusiveness, unity with nature and meets the requirements of cultural communication in the new era.

总之，该片是一部优秀的科普作品。在 CCTV-7 频道播出后，受到广大观众好评，整体制作水平国内领先。

In conclusion, the documentary is an excellent work on popular science and its overall production level takes the leading position in China. It is well received by the audience while broadcasting on CCTV-7.

建议：进一步修改完善，并译成外文，加大国内外宣传力度。

Suggestion: Have further modification and improvement, translate into foreign languages, and strengthen publicity from home and abroad.

评审组组长 / Leader of the review team:

Diao Xianmin

中国农业科学院作物科学研究所　　研究员

Researcher of Institute of Crop Science of Chinese Academy of Agricultural Sciences

副组长 / Vice leader:

Yang Tianyu

甘肃省农业科学院作物所　　研究员

Researcher of Institute of Crop Science of Gansu Academy of Agricultural Sciences

Feng Baili

西北农林科技大学　教授

Professor of Northwest Agriculture and Forestry University

评审组专家 /Experts of the review team:

沈　群　Shen Qun

中国农业大学　教授

Professor of China Agricultural University

管延安　Guan Yan'an

山东省农业科学院作物所　研究员

Researcher of Institute of Crop Science of Shandong Academy of Agricultural Sciences

陆　平　Lu Ping

中国农业科学院作物科学研究所　研究员

Researcher of Institute of Crop Science of Chinese Academy of Agricultural Sciences

原向阳　Yuan Xiangyang

山西农业大学　教授

Professor of Shanxi Agricultural University

郭二虎　Guo Erhu

山西省农业科学院作物所　研究员

Researcher of Institute of Crop Science of Shanxi Academy of Agricultural Sciences

刘金荣　Liu Jinrong

安阳市农业科学院　　研究员

Researcher of Anyang Academy of Agricultural Sciences

乔治军　Qiao Zhijun

山西省农业科学院　　研究员

Researcher of Shanxi Academy of Agricultural Sciences

程炳文　Cheng Bingwen

宁夏农林科学院固原分院　　研究员

Researcher of Guyuan Branch of Ningxia Academy of Agricultural Sciences

李书田　Li Shutian

赤峰市农牧科学院　　研究员

Researcher of Chifeng Academy of Agricultural and Husbandry Sciences

2019 年 1 月 4 日

January 4th, 2019

河北省老科学技术工作者协会评审意见
Review Comments from Hebei Association of Senior Scientists and Technologists

2019 年 1 月 13 日，河北省老科学技术工作者协会组成评审组，对河北省农林科学院与河北正奇文化传播有限公司等单位创作的《粟说——一粒小米的故事》纪录片进行了评审。评审组听取了策划、编导人员的工作汇报，观看了纪录片，经认真讨论，形成如下意见：

On January 13rd, 2019, Hebei Association of Senior Scientists and Technologists forms the review team for the evaluation of the documentary *The Story of a Millet* that is jointly produced by Hebei Academy of Agriculture and Forestry Sciences and Hebei Zhengqi Culture Communication Co. Ltd. The following remarks are given by the members of the review team after listening to the work report by the Planners and the Produce Directors, watching the documentary and having careful discussion:

1. 该片是首次以中国起源作物粟为专题拍摄的纪录片，具有拍摄时间长、采访地区广、采访人员结构全、涉及专业丰富等特点，素材丰富、内容翔实、画面真实，内容体现了科学性、真实性，具有重要的史料价值、科普价值和传播价值。

1. It is the first documentary to feature the foxtail millet, a crop of Chinese origin. This documentary has important historical, scientific and communication value due to its wide coverage of geographical areas and subjects, diversified interviewees, rich and detailed

materials, as well as the real pictures.

2. 该片从植物学、遗传育种学、考古学、历史学等多个角度考证了谷子起源于中国黄河流域，展示了其在中华农耕文明形成中的地位与作用，为观众了解中华文明发展历史提供了丰富的声像资料。

2. The documentary brings evidences from the view of botany, genetics, crop breeding, archaeology and history to show that the foxtail millet has originated in the Yellow River Basin of China and has important position and function in the formation of Chinese agricultural civilization, providing a wealth of audio-video information for the audience to understand the history of Chinese civilization development.

3. 该片普及了谷子的起源、进化与传播，谷子资源与育种创新，健康营养功能，精神文化内涵，深刻挖掘了谷子在中华民族优秀传统文化中所打下的物质、精神、文化、政治、科技、生态烙印，对粟文化传播、谷子产业发展、健康中国构建具有一定的指导意义。

3. The documentary has popularized the foxtail millet's origination, evolution, spreading, resource, breeding innovation, nutrition, health function and spiritual and cultural connotation, has deeply explored the material, spiritual, cultural, political, scientific and technological , ecological imprints that millet laid on the excellent traditional culture of the Chinese nation, which has a certain guiding significance for the millet culture popularization, millet industry development and Healthy China construction.

4. 该片遵循历史、现实、未来的逻辑思路，对谷子具有逆境抗争、环境友好、生态和谐、谦逊报恩、健康营养等特征进行了归纳，体现了中华民族所蕴含的不屈不挠、和谐共生、天人合一的精神实质，符合新时代文化传播要求。

4. The documentary, along the logical lines of history, reality and future, has summarized the millet's characteristics such as being resistant to stresses, friendly to environment, harmonious to ecology, modest and grateful, healthy and nutritious, reflecting the spirit of the Chinese nation of perseverance, inclusiveness, unity with nature and meets the requirements of cultural communication in the new era.

总之，该片是一部优秀的科普作品。在CCTV-7频道播出后，受到广大观众好评，整体制作水平居国内领先。

In conclusion, the documentary is an excellent work on popular science and its overall production level takes the leading position in China. It is well received by the audience while broadcasting on CCTV-7.

建议：进一步修改完善，争取在更多、更大平台播出，加大粟文化宣传力度。

Suggestion: Try to make it perfect and show on more and larger platforms so as to enhance the spreading of millet culture.

评审组组长／Leader of the review team:

Zang Shengye

中国老科学技术工作者协会　　副会长

Vice President of China Association of Senior Scientists and Technologists

河北省老科学技术工作者协会　　会长

President of Hebei Association of Senior Scientists and Technologists

评审组专家/Experts of review team:

唐树钰　Tang Shuyu

河北省老科学技术工作者协会　　常务副会长

Executive Vice President of Hebei Association of Senior Scientists and Technologists

张文军　Zhang Wenjun

河北省老科学技术工作者协会　　副会长

Vice President of Hebei Association of Senior Scientists and Technologists

刘秀华　Liu Xiuhua

河北省老科学技术工作者协会　　副会长

Vice President of Hebei Association of Senior Scientists and Technologists

田魁祥　Tian Kuixiang

河北省老科学技术工作者协会　　副会长

Vice President of Hebei Association of Senior Scientists and Technologists

王建军　Wang Jianjun

河北省老科学技术工作者协会　　秘书长

Secretary General of Hebei Association of Senior Scientists and Technologists

郑彦平　Zheng Yanping

河北省老科学技术工作者协会河北省农林科学院分会　　会长

President of Hebei Academy of Agriculture and Forestry Sciences branch of Hebei Association of Senior Scientists and Technologists

崔新明　Cui Xinming

河北省老科学技术工作者协会　　秘书长

Secretary General of Hebei Association of Senior Scientists and Technologists

王　旗　Wang Qi

河北省农业农村厅

Department of Agriculture and Rural Affairs of Hebei Province

尤栓庆　You Shuanqing

石家庄市鹿泉区政协　　原主席

Former Chairman of Luquan District's Political Consultative Conference

李彦平　Li Yanping

河北佛光山旅游景区　　董事长

Chairman of Hebei Foguang Mountain Tourism Area

2019 年 1 月 13 日

January 13rd, 2019

代序 1

Preface 1

粟是中国古代最重要的粮食作物，位居五谷之首。在漫长的农耕文明时代，中国人最大的梦想便是国泰民安、五谷丰登，而五谷中最早为中华先民所熟悉的便是粟与黍。江山社稷中的"稷"就来源于谷子，进而代指主管粮食丰歉的谷神。在史前新石器时代，华夏祖先已经开始大面积种植并食用粟和黍了。之后经过数千年的人工培育选种，中国培育出了异彩纷呈的粟类作物品种。中国最早的酒、醋就是用小米酿造的。在小麦传入中国、水稻跨越长江进入黄河流域之前的数千年中，正是粟与黍等带有颖壳的本土作物养育了中华民族，滋养了华夏文明，终使华夏文明成为同时代最辉煌的古代文明之一，且生息绵延数千载依然灿烂辉煌。可以说，在各种农作物当中，粟的文化内涵最为悠久丰富。粟文化这一座沉睡在地下的"金矿"等待着人们去挖掘。

Millet, the most important grain crop in ancient China, ranks the first in the five cereal crops. In the long period of agricultural civilization, the greatest dream of the Chinese people is that the country is peaceful, the people are safe and prosperous and the land abounds with bumper harvest. Among the five cereals, millet is the earliest crop to be familiar to the Chinese ancestors. The "Ji" of Jiangshan Sheji (the whole country) is derived from millet which refers to the grain God who is in charge of abundant grain. In the prehistoric Neolithic age, Chinese ancestors began to plant millet on a large scale and eat it. After thousands of years of artificial cultivation and selection, China has cultivated various kinds of millet cultivars. The earliest wine and vinegar in China was made from millet. In the thousands of years before wheat was introduced into China and rice crossed the Yangtze River into the Yellow River Basin, it was millet that nurtured the Chinese nation and nourished Chinese civilization, which eventually made the Chinese civilization one of the most brilliant ancient civilizations of the same time, and it has been living for thousands of years and still brilliant. It can be said that among all kinds of crops, millet has the longest and the most profound cultural connotation. Millet culture, a sleeping "gold mine", is waiting for people to excavate.

尽管粟文化研究是一个极具价值的研究课题，然而，长期以来其被学术界忽视。部分原因在于，在生产力水平极低的年代，粟乃至五谷仅仅是解决国民温饱的手段，粟文化的研究与弘扬难以提上日程。随着全面建设小康社会时代的到来，粟作中蕴含的历史文化和人文精神日益凸增，迫切需要对其进行深入挖掘和大力宣传。《中国粟文化研究》从选题上具有填补空白的意义，其出版恰逢其时。

Although the study on millet culture is a valuable research topic, it has been ignored by the academic community for a long time. Part of the reason is that in the era of extremely low productivity, millet, even the five cereals, is only a means to solve the national food and clothing, so it is difficult to put the research and promotion of millet culture on the agenda. With the arrival of the era of building a well-off society in an all-round way, the historical culture and humanity contained in millet cultivation are increasing day by day. It is urgent to excavate and publicize it. The *Research on Chinese Millet Culture* has the significance of filling in the blank from the topic selection, and its publication is just in time.

《黄帝内经》提出了"五谷为养，五果为助，五畜为益，五菜为充"的膳食配伍原则，祖国医学素来有"五谷养五脏"的说法。国人几千年来一直把谷物当作主食，被证明是符合养生之道的。然而，小米逐渐成为一种"杂粮"，成为继精米白面之后的一种调剂。东方民族饮食西方化会导致"三高"等"富贵病"增多。一方水土养一方人，韩国人"身土不二"的策略启示我们，恢复"五谷为养"的优良饮食传统，是国民健康的不二选择。使粟重新成为中国人餐桌上的主食，必须通过文化引领，创造需求，培育需求，打造品牌。大力宣传粟文化，把文化元素注入五谷杂粮之中，满足人们的口福、眼福，既是杂粮产业发展的重要方向，也是我国农业现代化的重要使命。在《中国粟文化研究》基础上，作者又协同文化传播公司制作了四集纪录片《粟说——一粒小米的故事》，为作物科普性读物，对粟文化的传承与发展发挥了很好的作用。

Huangdi's Classic of Internal Medicine puts forward the principle of dietary compatibility of "the five cereals for cultivation, five fruits for help, five livestock for benefit, and five vegetables for filling". Traditional Chinese medicine has long created the theory of "the five cereals nourish five internal organs". For thousands of years, Chinese people have been taking grain as their main food, which has proved to be in line with the principle of health. However, millet has gradually become a kind of "miscellaneous grain corps", which has become a kind of adjustment after wheat flour and polished rice. The inevitable result of the Westernization of the Oriental diet is that the "three highs" and other "illness of affluence" are increasing day by day. Each place has its streams in from all over the country, the Korean people's strategy of "integrate the body and the land" enlightens us that the only choice for us to keep health is to restore the fine diet tradition of "the five cereals for food". In order to make millet the staple food on the Chinese dining table again, we must build a brand under the guidance of culture and create and cultivate demand. It is not only an important direction for the development of grain crops industry, but also a significant mission of China's agricultural modernization to vigorously publicize millet culture and inject cultural elements into the five cereals and grains to meet people's oral and eye blessings. On the basis of *Research on Chinese Millet Culture*, the authors, in collaboration with the cultural communication company, produced four episodes of documentary *The Story of a Millet*, which played a considerable role in the inheritance and development of millet culture.

《中国粟文化研究》与《粟说——一粒小米的故事》从研究和普及两个层面对粟文化的挖掘、传承与发展做了许多开拓性的研究。它将分散在历史学、人类学、农业经济管理学等学科的粟文化资源进行系统集成，首次从物质、精神、制度和生态四个层面全面挖掘了粟文化的丰富内涵，阐明了粟文化在中华民族传统文化体系中的重要地位；首次从经济价值、社会价值和生态价值三方面分析了传统粟文化在当代社会的价值，提出了企业、政府等多主体参与的粟文化传承与发展途径。这些内容和观点颇具创新性。

The *Research on Chinese Millet Culture* and *The Story of a Millet* made a lot of pioneering research on the excavation, inheritance and development of millet culture from two aspects of research and popularization. It systematically integrates the millet culture resources scattered in history, anthropology, agricultural economic management and other disciplines. For the first time, it comprehensively excavates the rich connotation of millet culture from four aspects of material, spirit, system and ecology, and clarifies the crucial position of millet culture in the traditional Chinese culture system. It is the first time to analyze the value of traditional millet culture in contemporary society from three aspects of economic value, social value and ecological value, and put forward the inheritance and development methodology of millet culture with the joint participation of enterprises and governments. These contents and perspectives are quite innovative.

作为一项关系中华民族软实力的重大课题，对粟文化的研究需要协调组织不同学科领域的学者参与。只有将考古学、农学、植物学、遗传学、生态学、历史学、经济地理学、民族学等学科领域的理论、研究方法结合起来，才能真正实现多学科的整合研究。我相信，粟文化研究作为一个新的学术增长点，必将引起更多学者的关注和积极参与；粟文化作为中华民族文化软实力的重要组成部分，必将得到社会各界的大力支持，共同为推动中华民族的伟大复兴奠定坚实的文化基础。

The study, as a major subject related to the soft power of the Chinese nation on millet culture, is required to coordinate and organize scholars from different disciplines to take part in, and combine the theories and research methodologies of archaeology, agronomy, botany, genetics, ecology, history, economic geography, ethnology and other disciplines, thereby achieving the integrated study of multiple disciplines. I believe that as a new academic growing point, the study on millet culture will surely attract more scholars' attention and proactive participation; as a component of great importance of the soft power of Chinese culture, millet culture is bound to enjoy support from all walks of life and jointly lay a solid cultural foundation for promoting the great rejuvenation of the Chinese nation.

中国工程院副院长、院士　刘旭

Vice President and Academician of the Chinese Academy of Engineering　Liu Xu

2020 年 8 月

August 2020

代序 2

Preface 2

　　近得张云、王慧军合著的《中国粟文化研究》（中国农业科学技术出版社，2014）。灯下品读，所获良多。兹将心得列陈，与同道共享。全书共立七章，始自粟之起源，继述粟作农事、粟米典章、祭祀习俗、粟作生态、当代粟文化，挂笔于粟文化发展构想。单从这个目录，即可窥见该书文理兼济，古今咸备的特点。

Recently, I had the chance to access to *Research on Chinese Millet Culture* co-authored by Zhang Yun and Wang Huijun (China Agricultural Science and Technology Press, 2014). I have read it at night and acquired a lot. I would like to share what I have learnt with readers. The book consists of seven chapters, namely the origin of millet, millet farming, millet laws, sacrificial customs, millet cultivation ecology, contemporary millet culture, and the development concept of millet culture. The aforementioned contents could reflect the arts and science, ancient and modern features of the book.

　　作者对我国的粟历史、粟文化、粟生态和粟价值作了独到的阐述。该书将我国数千年来有关粟的种植、加工、食用及与之相伴而出的典章制度、习俗观念、典故辞赋、礼仪伦理等统称粟文化。这是一个历史悠远而内容庞大的文化系统。欲将这个复杂系统架构于一部学术专著之中，需要具备农史学、人类学、社会学、经济学等学科的理论知识，需要掌握考古学、历史学、文字学的文献史料，还需要熟悉当代粟作的科技、产业、市场、文化的现状和趋势。由于责之甚多，成之甚难，是故学术界避之者也多，迄今未见粟史专著面世。此题空置累年，虚位求贤。两位作者毅然为文脉填空白，奋力而成大作。后稷得传人，粟作添华章，至为可敬可嘉，令人欣慰欣喜。

The authors have expressed a unique elaboration of China's millet history, culture, ecology and value. The planting, processing and consumption of millet in China for thousands of years, as well as the related laws, regulations, customs, allusions, poetry, prose, etiquette and ethic, are collectively referred to as the millet culture in the book, which represents a cultural system with a long history and enormous contents. The construction of this complicated system in the academic monograph requires being equipped with theoretical knowledge of agricultural history, anthropology, sociology, economics and other disciplines, mastering documentary sources of archaeology, history and philology, and being acquainted with the current status and trend of science and technology, industry, market and culture of contemporary millet cultivation. The majority of scholars avoid involving in the above-mentioned study, behind which is the abundance of responsibilities and challenges. No monograph on millet history has been published until this book appears. This topic has been vacant for many years, which requires talents to break through. It is gratifying that the two authors resolutely filled in the gaps and spared no effort to accomplish such a masterpiece. The descendants of Houji (The Chinese ancestor of agriculture) who flourish the millet cultivation are the most honorable and commendable.

中华民族是最仰赖"粒食"的民族。大多数国人以谷物为主食，以至进餐直接就说"吃饭"。因此，自古以来，人们对粮食作物都极为重视，尤其擅长品种选育。中华文明最早发源于黄河流域，而此流域适宜粟类作物的种植。早期的典籍文献中，反映粟文化的史料特别集中而丰富。

The Chinese nation represents the one that relies most on "grain". Most Chinese people live on grain, so they would like to use the expression of "eating grains" instead of "eating a meal". Therefore, since ancient times, people have attached great importance to grain crops, especially have been adept at crop breeding. Chinese civilization originated from the Yellow River basin, where millet crops grow well. In the early ancient books and record documents, there exist concentrated and plentiful historical materials reflecting millet culture.

《诗经·大雅·生民》说："诞后稷之穑，有相之道，弗厥丰草，种之黄茂，实方实苞"。这里的"种之黄茂，实方实苞"，讲的就是粟类作物的选种。"黄茂"是光润美好，"方"是硕大，"苞"是饱满或充满活力。选穗大的、饱满的做种子，这是对良种的具体要求。这说明西周时代已明确形成粟良种的概念，并出现了不同的品种类型。《吕氏春秋•任地》更是具体提出了粟良种的要求："使藁数节而茎坚""使穗大而坚匀""使粟圆而薄糠""使米多沃而食之强"等。这就是说，一个好的"粟"品种应当具备：植株茎秆健壮，穗大而饱满，籽粒出米率高，米质优良，饭食口感好等优点。《齐民要术》是古代论述粟类作物最为详备的农书："凡谷，成熟有早晚，苗秆有高下，收实有多少，质性有强弱，米味有美恶，粒实有息耗"。这表明北魏时期已经从成熟期、植株高矮、产量品质及其种质遗传特性和适应性能等方面，相当全面地评价一个粟品种。这些珍贵的史料为研究粟文化提供了便利的条件。

The *Book of Poetry: The First Birth of Major Odes* states: "Houji would farm in his own way, at the proper time of a day. He cleared away the rampant weeds and sowed the choicest millet seeds. The seedlings in the soil would sprout". "He sowed the choicest millet seeds. The seedlings in the soil would sprout" refers to the selection of millet crops. "Huangmao" means glossy and beautiful, "Fang" means large, and "Bao" means plump or full of vitality. The fine breeding concretely means large and plump seeds, indicating that the concept of millet breeding has been clearly formed in the Western Zhou Dynasty, with the emergence of diverse types of varieties. *Lüshi Chunqiu: Rendi* has specifically put forward the requirements of fine millet cultivars: "with several stem joints and the strong roots" "large and even spike" "round millet and thin chaff" "palatable grain and favorable taste", etc. In other words, a fine "millet" cultivar should be featured by strong stem, large and plump spike, sound grain yield, favorable quality, favorable taste, etc. *Qimin Yaoshu* stands for the most detailed agricultural book on millet crops in ancient times: "In the millet cultivation, there always exists early or late maturation, high or short seedling stalks, plenteous or poor harvest, sound or poor quality, favorable or poor taste, and plump or shrivelled spike." This manifests that people could quite comprehensively evaluate the millet cultivar in terms of its maturity, crop height, yield and quality, germplasm characteristics and adaptability in the Northern Wei Dynasty. These precious historical materials have facilitated the millet culture study.

一万多年前全球气候变暖，人类为应对生存压力而发明了农业。农业的产生，推动以籽粒大小均匀的黍米来制订大小测量方法。以至康熙皇帝都说："固知昔人之定分寸，度空径，独有取于黍者。五谷惟黍粒均齐，余则不能无大小之故也。"至于与粟、黍、禾、稷等有关的成语短语，书中也不惜篇幅，罗列毕至，把一部艰涩难读的学术专著写得文思涌动，妙趣横生。

More than 10,000 years ago, due to the global warming, human beings had to develop agriculture to cope with the survival stresses. The emergence of agriculture has promoted the formulation of rice with equal grain size. Even Emperor Kangxi of Qing Dynasty said: "It is known that our ancestors used millet to identify sizes and measure pore sizes. Only grains of the millet among the five cereals are even, and the rest are of different sizes". As for the idioms and phrases related to millet, the authors have spent a great effort to list with a huge length, which makes an obscure and difficult academic monograph full of literary and interesting ideas.

《中国粟文化研究》除了对粟作技术与生产经验作了考辨论说之外，还对与粟相关的典章制度、文化习俗作了广泛的搜罗汇集，令人信服地揭示了粟文化在中国传统文化中的深刻印记。这些由粟衍生出来的文化智慧，渗透到传统文化的方方面面，在今天依然能够给人以启示。例如，积粟防灾、人粟拜爵、黄粱一梦、斗粟尺布、辞金受粟等的典章典故，读之如饮甘泉食粱饴，既解文化之渴，又充知识之餐。作者还指出，我国古代度量衡的规制，最初都是人类社会的一系列重大进步，完成了从"生态利用"到"生态改造"的飞跃。粟和黍的野生种因抗逆性强、生育期短的特性，成为中华民族首选的栽培作物。驯化粟、黍是中国北方原始农业的开端。由于北方地区冬长夏短，来源于野生动植物的食物容易出现季节性匮乏，迫使北方人民更早形成完善的农业生产体系，以养活不断膨胀的人口。因此，北方粟作农业的发展进程比南方稻作农业的发展进程要快，粟文化的发展水平也在长时期内高于稻文化。

In addition to the research on millet cultivation technology and production experience, the *Research on Chinese Millet Culture* also makes a comprehensive collection of relevant laws and regulations, cultural customs, revealing the profound imprint of millet culture in Chinese traditional culture in a convincing way. These cultural wisdom, derived from millet, permeates all aspects of traditional culture and can still enlighten people today. For example, the allusions such as accumulating millet for disaster prevention, importing millet into the government in exchange for a position, a golden millet dream, brothers at loggerheads, and rejecting money while accepting the millet are read as if drinking sweet spring and eating sorghum, which can not only satisfy the thirst of culture, but also fill the meal of knowledge. The authors also pointed out that the regulation of weights and measures in ancient China was a series of crucial progress in human society, which completed the leap from "ecological utilization" to "ecological transformation". Because of their strong stress resistance and short growth period, millets have become the preferred cultivated crops for the Chinese nation. Domestication of millet symbolized the beginning of primitive agriculture in Northern China. Due to the long winter and short summer in this area, food from wild animals and crops is prone to seasonal shortage, forcing the northern people to turn to acclimation of crops, which contributed to accumulation of profound knowledge. As a consequence, the development course of millet farming in the North of China is faster than that of rice farming in the South of China, and the development level of millet culture is higher than that of rice culture for a long time.

更为可贵的是，作者一改述古溺古、恋古忘今的学界积弊，真正做到了以古鉴今，古为今用。该书专辟两章，讨论粟文化的当代价值和粟文化发展构想。面对现实，条陈理析，其中多有真知灼见，入木三分者。这些针对当代粟作的论述，上可献国是，下可开民智，为粟产业的兴旺，为粟文化的传承，至诚至虑，肝胆相映。

What's more valuable is that the authors changed the accumulated shortcomings of the academic circles which indulges in the past, prefer the past to the present, and implement the principle of learning from the past and make the past to serve the present. Two chapters are used in this book to discuss the contemporary value and development conception of millet culture. Many of these systematic opinions, in the face of reality, have deep and penetrating expression. These discourses on contemporary millet production can contribute to the country, widen the horizon of the people, devoted to the prosperity of millet industry and the inheritance of millet culture.

曾几何时，我们称粟为小米，而大家的餐桌上通常也少了一些小米。这可能不是慰人的"粟错"、自谦的"粟成"，对人对己，专取粟之"小"。然而在古代，粟可大到与江山社稷齐列，四民不可须臾或缺。粟滋养了中华民族与中华文明，在政治、经济、文化等方面都产生了深远的影响。甚至在抗日战争及解放战争期间，"小米加步枪"书写过世界军事史上的辉煌。岁月的变迁使我们与过往的联系越来越疏离，忙碌的身影使我们对"根文化"越来越模糊。挖掘与传承粟文化，不只是学者的使命，也是我们民族的期望。

Once upon a time, we called millet as Xiaomi (small grains), and millet was usually indispensable on the table at home. This may not be a "millet Cuo" (minor mistakes) to comfort people, a modest word "millet Cheng". The meaning of "small" of millet is often used in describing ourselves or other people. However, in ancient times, millet could be as big as the country, and the four social strata were also indispensable. Millet nourishes the Chinese nation and Chinese civilization, and exerts far-reaching influence on politics, economy, culture and so on. Even during the War of Resistance against Japan and the War of Liberation in modern times, "Millet plus Rifle" forged glories in the world military history. The change of time alienates us more and more from the past, and the fast pace of life makes us more and more vague about the "root culture". Exploring and inheriting millet culture is not only the mission of scholars, but also the expectation of our nation.

为了更好地传播和普及粟文化，作者协同文化传播公司改编学术专著，又用了四年时间拍摄了四集纪录片《粟说——一粒小米的故事》，面向不同层次读者与观众，这一贡献，对国家，对粟，对文化，对研究，对宣传，对产业振兴善莫大焉。

In order to better spread and popularize the millet culture, the authors, in collaboration with the cultural communication company, adapted the academic monograph and spent four years filming four episodes of documentary *The Story of a Millet* which aims at various levels of readers. Its contribution is of great significance to the country, the millet, the culture, the research, the publicity and the revitalization of the industry.

中国农史学会会长　曹幸穗

President of China Agricultural History Association　Cao Xingsui

2020 年 8 月

August 2020

代序 3

Preface 3

谷子是起源于我国的古老农作物，是中华民族的哺育作物、新中国的缔造作物。围绕谷子、糜子等粟类作物的生产、加工和食用，衍生出"粟文化"这一概念，它是中华农耕文明的源头，同时，是中华文明起源的重要文化根基。因此，粟文化的研究与普及在我国具有多方面的重要意义。

Millet represents an ancient crop originated from China, feeding the Chinese nation and establishing the new China. The concept of "millet culture", derived from the production, processing and consumption of millet crops such as foxtail millet and proso millet, is the source of both Chinese agricultural civilization and the vital cultural foundation of Chinese civilization. Therefore, the research and popularization of millet culture are of great multi-aspect significance in our country.

谷子不仅在中国文明发展史上有重要作用，而且在三千多年以前传到欧洲等世界各地，对世界其他地区的文明发展也做出了重要贡献，从这个意义上说，对粟文化的研究既是中国的，也是世界的。历史上很长时期内，中国的南稻北粟构成了中国农耕文明格局的重要特点，而粟文化的影响和意义远远超过稻文化。然而，由于种种原因，稻文化研究者众多，《中国稻作文化史》等重量级的专著早已问世，而粟文化的研究者寥寥，至今尚未有专著出版。本书填补了我国关于粟文化的专著空白，不但在国内处于先进水平，而且在世界上是独一无二的。

  Millet not only plays a crucial role in the history of Chinese civilization development, but also has been spread to Europe and other parts of the world more than 3,000 years ago, making indispensible contributions to the development of civilization in the rest of the world. In this sense, the study of millet culture is a matter for China and as well as the world. For a long period of history, the model of "rice in the South of China and millet in the North of China" stands for an important feature of China's agricultural civilization pattern, however, the influence and significance of millet culture far exceeds that of rice culture. Due to various reasons, there exists a pile of researchers on rice culture, with *History of Chinese Rice Culture* and other heavyweight monographs being published, while few researchers on millet culture have published nothing so far. This book has bridged the gap in China's monograph on millet culture, which not only represents an advanced monograph in China, but also a unique one in the world.

  谷子的驯化在距今 10500 年左右的新石器时代晚期，夏商以来一直是中国的主要粮食和饲草作物。20 世纪 50 至 70 年代，我国谷子播种面积达 1 亿亩[①]以上，曾是我国北方的第三大粮食作物。然而，从 20 世纪 70 年代开始到 90 年代中后期，谷子的播种面积迅速萎缩，逐渐由全国主要粮食作物变为区域性重要作物，谷子科研也遇到了前所未有的挑战。在当时的历史形势下，广大谷子科研工作者没有气馁，他

---

① 1 亩 ≈ 666.7 平方米。

们为了使谷子这一中华民族的哺育作物重新焕发青春，付出了大量的心血和汗水。可以说，粟文化所蕴含的民族精神，是激励广大科研工作者的精神动力。

Domesticated in the late Neolithic Age about 10,500 years ago, millet has been the main grain and forage crop in China since Xia and Shang Dynasties. During the 1950s and 1970s, the seeded area of millet, which was once the third largest grain crop in northern China, reached more than 100 million mu[①] in China. However, from the 1970s to the middle and late 1990s, the seeded area of millet, which gradually converted from a national major grain crop into a regional crop, shrank rapidly, with the scientific research of millet encountering unprecedented challenges. Under the historical situation of the day, the millet researchers did not become discouraged and paid a lot of painstaking efforts and sweat to rejuvenate millet, the feeding crop of the Chinese nation. It can be put that the national spirit contained in millet culture represents the spiritual drive of the broad masses of scientific researchers.

针对谷子产业的历史与现状，我曾进行深刻的反思，并于2007年提出"用粟文化发展谷子产业"这一命题。2008年谷子被列入国家现代农业产业技术体系，而粟文化无疑是谷子糜子产业技术体系的特点和亮点所在。作为谷子糜子产业技术体系的首席科学家，我曾多次同王慧军教授就粟文化这一论题进行讨论。他作为产业经济岗位的科学家，对此深感兴趣，并将此选题向张云博士后进行推介。之后，

① 1 mu ≈ 666.7 m^2。

两位作者便着手收集资料，历时三年研究，拿出了沉甸甸的研究报告。当我欣喜地打开这本专著的电子版时，心情就像看到了一个谷子新品种的育成一样兴奋激动。

In view of the history and current status of millet industry, I have contemplated profoundly and put forward the proposition of "developing millet industry with millet culture" in 2007. Millet was enrolled in the national modern agricultural industry technology system in 2008. Undoubtedly, the millet culture stands for the features and highlights of the millet industry technology system. As the Chief Scientist of the millet industry technology system, I have repeatedly discussed the millet culture with Professor Wang Huijun. As a post scientist in the industrial economy, he was deeply interested in this proposition and introduced it to his Postdoc Zhang Yun. Since then, the two authors commenced collecting information, which lasted for three years and produced a meaningful study report. When I opened up the electronic version of this monograph with joy, I was as thrilled as seeing the success of a newly bred millet variety.

本书至少有三大特点令我眼前一亮：一是在选题上，它首次对粟文化的历史、内涵与当代价值进行了系统挖掘与全面表述，填补了粟文化的研究空白。二是它面向应用，体系完整。作者遵循历史→现实→未来的逻辑思路，在简要回顾了粟作史之后，着重从物质、制度、精神和生态四个层面总结粟文化的丰富内涵，从经济价值、社会价值和生态价值三方面分析了传统粟文化在当代社会的价值，继而展望未来，提出了粟文化传承与发展的系统构想。三个时空维度的分析有机地结合起来，使本书不再是纯学术性的农史著作，而是成为一本古为今用、颇具应用价值的论著。三是多视角多学科的研究方法。该书将农学理论与农业经济管理学等多学科紧密结合起来，从供给和需求两个角度剖析了谷子种植面积衰退的原因，提出了多功能农业时代谷子产业与粟文化融合发展的建议。我认为这一论断抓住了谷子产业的关键所在，体现出了粟文化的广阔应用前景。

What impressed me deeply are that at least three striking features in this book: Firstly, its topic is the first to systematically excavate and comprehensively express the history, connotation and contemporary value of the millet culture, which has filled the gap of millet culture research. Secondly, it is practice-oriented with a complete structure. Following the logic of "history → reality → future", after a brief review of the millet production history, the authors summarized the abundant connotation of millet culture from four aspects, namely substance, system, spirit and ecology, analyzed the value of traditional millet culture in modern society from three aspects of economic, social and ecological value, and prospectively put forward a systematic conception of millet culture inheritance and development. Through the analytical intergration of the three spatial and temporal dimensions, this book is no longer a purely academic work on agricultural history, but a treatise of great application value that adapts ancient forms for present-day use. The third feature is its multi-perspective and multi-disciplinary research methodology. With the close combination of agronomy theory, agricultural economic management and other disciplines, the book dissects the reasons for the recession of the millet planting area from the perspectives of supply and demand, and proposes the integrated development of millet industry and culture in the era of multi-functional agriculture. This inference has taken hold of the key point of millet industry and reflected the broad application prospect of millet culture.

作者在《中国粟文化研究》专著的基础上，协同文化传播公司又制作了四集纪录片《粟说——一粒小米的故事》，后者作为普及版本，扩大了读者对象范围，面向了不同层次的读者。我相信，本书能激起广大普通读者的阅读兴趣，毕竟我国是一个"民以食为天"的国度，当农业的温饱功能基本满足之后，其文化传承功能日益凸显出来，《舌尖上的中国》等电视纪录片的热播就是一个典型体现。本书作为中国五谷文化研究的一个重要组成部分，供广大读者在茶余饭后阅读，一定会增强他们在消费谷子产品过程中的趣味性，从而潜移默化地提高粟文化在大众中的影响力。

On the basis of the monograph *Research on Chinese Millet Culture*, the authors, in collaboration with the Cultural Communication Company, has produced another four-episode documentary *The Story of a Millet,* which acts as a popular version, aimed at a wider range of readers. The book could arouse the reading interests of ordinary readers, as China is on earth a country where "hunger breeds discontentment". The cultural inheritance function of agriculture would become increasingly prominent with its subsistence function basically satisfied, the typical embodiment of which is the hit TV documentary, *A Bite of China*. As an important part of the study of China's five cereals culture, this book is suitable at readers' leisure, which will definitely enhance their interests in the process of consuming millet products, thus imperceptibly boosting the influence of millet culture among the public.

国家谷子糜子产业技术体系首席科学家　刁现民

Chief Scientist of the National Millet Industry Technology System　Diao Xianmin

2020 年 8 月

August 2020

一粒小米的故事
The story of a millet

主编寄语 / Editor's note

王慧军 / 河北省农林科学院　原院长

Professor Wang Huijun, Former President, Hebei Academy of Agriculture and Forestry Sciences

以小米为代表的粟类作物，起源于我们国家，是我们中华民族的哺育作物，也是我们国家农耕文明的源头。小米所具有的逆境抗争、环境友好、生态和谐、谦逊报恩、健康营养等特性，是我们国家优秀传统文化的标志。

Millet crops, originated from China, have been feeding Chinese , and also created the farming civilization in China. The characters of millet, such as resistance to stresses, environment friendly, ecological harmony, humility and gratitude, healthy and nutritious, are the symbols of Chinese excellent traditional culture.

要讲好中国故事，提升我们的文化自信，应该挖掘小米在中华文明的历史长河中所打下的物质、精神、政治、文化、生态烙印。知道它从哪里来要到哪里去，并向世界传播出去。

To tell a good Chinese story and enhance cultural confidence, we should excavate the physical, spiritual, political, cultural and ecological imprints that millet has laid in the long history of Chinese civilization. Knowing where it comes from and where it goes to, and spread it to the world.

这就是我们所讲的小米的故事，也是中华民族的故事！

This is the story of millet and the story of the Chinese nation.

创作团队手记
Notes form the Production Crew

从天山脚下到茫茫草原，

从西南苗寨的青山翠谷，

到黄土高原的辽阔苍黄，

我们追随着粟的来历，

见证粟与中华民族的相依相伴！

From the foot of Tianshan Mountain to the vast

grassland,from the green hills and valleys of Hmong Village

in southwest China to the broad Loess Plateau in northwest,

we follow the origin of millet and witness its interdependence

with the Chinese nation.

粟说
一粒小米的故事
The story of a millet

记录种子的萌发，

等待花的绽放，

感受型的变化，味的调和。

聆听粟于中华民族的心灵共鸣！

穿越半个中国，行程30000千米，我们在追溯一粒小米的故事。

Record the sprouting of seeds, wait for the blooming of flowers, feel the changing of shapes and the harmony of taste. Listen to the soul resonance of the Chinese nation. Traveling 30,000 kilometers across half of China, we are tracing a story about millet.

I 粟源
Source of Millet

II

粟种
Seeds of Millet

III 粟味
Flavor of Millet

IV

粟魂
Soul of Millet

粟说

一粒小米的故事

The story of a millet

I 粟 源

Episode I
Source of Millet

粟，在中华文明发展的历史长河中，留下了深刻的烙印。从某种意义上说，这是历史的选择，也是中华民族的选择。粟，也因此成为江山社稷的象征。

Millet crop has left a deep imprint in the long history of Chinese civilization's development. In a sense, this is the choice of history and the choice of the Chinese nation. Millet, therefore, has become a symbol of our society and nation.

刘旭 / 中国工程院　院士

Academician Liu Xu, Chinese Academy of Engineering

引 言 / Introduction

　　一株野草，因为人的选择，而开始蜕变。一粒种子，虽然渺小，萌发出的力量却如此巨大。它从大河之滨，跨越山川的阻碍，传播到四面八方。它是黄河流域农耕时代的开始，农业文明的发端；它的历史，湮没在岁月的长河之中，因时光的冲刷而略显斑驳，但依旧熠熠生辉。这是一粒米的故事，也是中华民族的故事。

狗尾草 / Bristlegrass

A weed begins to metamorphose because of human selection. A small seed sprouts so much power. It crosses the obstacles of mountains and rivers and spreads to all directions, which was the beginning of the agrarian age and civilization in the Yellow River Basin. Its history, annihilated in the long river of years, experienced ups and downs of time, but still shining. This is a story of millet, a story of Chinese nation.

谷子 / Millet

小米的秘密 / The secret of millet

粟，在中国北方通称谷子，籽实去壳以后，叫作小米。谷子耐旱、抗贫瘠，生产相同重量的粮食，谷子的需水量只有玉米的 1/3、小麦的 1/2、水稻的 1/5。但在今天，小米并非中国人的主粮，然而，令人惊奇的是，中国几乎所有的省份，都能看到谷子的踪迹。中国人从什么时候开始种植谷子？一种边缘化的小宗作物，为什么在中国境内有如此广泛的分布？这里面，究竟隐藏着怎样的秘密？

Millet crops, generally known as foxtail millet and proso millet, sometimes also known as "Su". Millet is drought and poor soil tolerance. The water demand of millet is only 1/3 of corn, 1/2 of wheat and 1/5 of rice by producing the same weight of grain. Nowadays, millet is not the staple food among Chinese. However, millet can be surprisingly traced in almost all regions in China. When did the Chinese begin to grow millet? Why was a marginalized crop so widely distributed in China? What was the secret behind?

天刚亮，苏志文老两口就下地了。谷子，是魏塔村的主要作物。这里的年降雨量不足 300 毫米。前几天刚下了一场雨，趁着墒情合适，老苏要抓紧播种。

6

At dawn, Su Zhiwen and his wife went to the fields. Millet is the main crop in Weita Village. The annual precipitation here is less than 300 mm. Days ago, it rained. Su should sow the seeds quickly while the soil moisture was still maintained.

陕西省　延安市安塞区魏塔村
Weita village, Ansai district, Yan'an City, Shaanxi Province

苏志文 / Su Zhiwen

与粟作同生的伟大发明

A great invention of symbiosis with millet

这里依旧保留着古老的农具和传统的耕作模式。牛耕和铁犁，出现于公元前 6 世纪，伴随着铁犁牛耕的出现，中国人开始走向精耕细作的道路。在黄土高原上，还保留着另外一种古老的播种方式。

They keep using ancient farming tools with traditional farming patterns. Cattle farming and iron plow first appeared in the 6th century B.C. With the emergence of Cattle farming and iron plow, Chinese began intensive farming. On the Loess Plateau, there is another ancient way of sowing.

甘肃省　白银市会宁县 / Huining County, Baiyin City, Gansu Province

耧车，发明于公元前 2 世纪的西汉时期，是现代播种机的始祖。铁犁牛耕和耧车，是中国对于世界农业的重要贡献。这些伟大的发明，都是伴随着粟作而生。

The cart, invented in the 2nd century B.C., is the ancestor of the modern seeder. Iron plow, cattle farming and cart sowing are important contributions of China to world agriculture. These great inventions were born with millet crops.

楼车 / Cart

铁犁牛耕 / Iron plow led by cattle

一大早，王怀英就和老伴赶到自家的地里间苗。间苗的同时，捎带锄第一遍草。锄草用的铁锄，发明于两千多年前的战国时期。一上午，王怀英和老伴只完成了3分地①。一千多年前，唐代诗人李绅，用"锄禾日当午，汗滴禾下土"这样的诗句，刻画着农人在田地里劳作的辛劳。禾，在中国古代专指一种作物，那就是谷子。

Early in the morning, Wang Huaiying and his wife rushed to their fields to thin the seedlings and take a hoe weeding for the first time. The iron hoe for weeding was invented more than two thousand years ago during the Warring States Period. The couple completed only 200m^2 in the whole morning. More than a thousand years ago, Tang Dynasty poet Li Shen depicted the farmer's hard work in the field with such poems as "Hoeing millet in mid-day heat, sweat dripping to the earth beneath". In ancient China, the crop specifically refers to millet, pronounced "he".

① 3分地 =200平方米。

禾与谷／"He" and millet

河北省　张家口市宣化区南庄子村
Nanzhuangzi Village,Xuanhua district, Zhangjiakou City, Hebei Province

王怀英和妻子
Wang Huaiying and his wife

米与粟 / "Mi" and millet

殷墟，出土过举世闻名的甲骨文。甲骨文，距今已有3600多年的历史。在甲骨文中，"禾"字，就是一株谷子的全貌。而甲骨文中的"米"字，像是一个结满籽粒的谷穗。公元100年，东汉文学家许慎编著的《说文解字》，是中国最古老的字典。里面对"米"字进行了更为明晰的解读：米，粟实也，象禾实之形。意为：米是粟的籽实，字形像谷子结实的形状。种种迹象，都在吐露出一些秘密，即粟对于中国的影响，似乎远远超过普通人的想象。

The world famous Oracle, with a history of more than 3600 years, was unearthed in Yin xu. In Oracle, the shape of word "he" is the panorama of a millet plant, while the shape of word "mi" likes a spike full of grains. In 100 A.D., *Shuowen Jiezi*, compiled by Xu Shen, a writer of the Eastern Han Dynasty, is the oldest dictionary in China. There is a clearer interpretation of the word "mi": the seed of millet, its zigzag shape is like the gathering millet spikes. All sorts of signs are revealing some secrets. The influence of millet on China seems to be far beyond ordinary people's imagination.

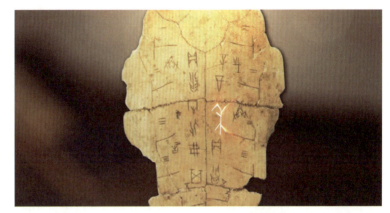

甲骨文 / Oracle inscription

河南省　安阳市殷墟 / Yinxu, Anyang City, Henan Province

小米种植合作社社长刘海庆，在网上发帖，招募全国各地的大学生，参加他举办的夏令营活动。

Liu Haiqing, Head of Millet Planting Cooperative, posted online to recruit college students from all over the country to participate in his summer camp activities.

让这些大学生把这里的小米文化带出去，让更多的人知道。

Let these college students propagate the millet culture and inform more people know.

刘海庆 / Liu Haiqing

刘海庆 / 小米合作社　社长
Liu Haiqing, Head of Millet Planting Cooperative

关于小米，人们更熟悉的或许是宋真宗赵恒《劝学诗》中"书中自有千钟粟"之句。千钟粟代表着远大前程。而对于刘海庆来说，他想的更多的是小米的销售前景。刘海庆将带领这些大学生，徒步前往敖汉旗东部的新石器时代遗址——兴隆沟遗址。

As for millet, perhaps people are more familiar with the phrase "Reading brings us plenty of millets" in Emperor of Song Dynasty Zhao Heng's poems of *Persuasion to Learn*. Plenty of millets represent a great future. For Liu Haiqing, what he thinks important is the high profit and price of millet. Liu Haiqing will lead the students to Xinglonggou, a Neolithic site in the eastern part of Aohan Banner.

兴隆沟遗址 / Xinglonggou site

碳化粟 / Carbonized millet

巨大的开阔土地上，一个个灰黑色的土圈，引起了大学生们的注意。这些土圈，是距今大约 8000 年前的新石器时代，中华先民在敖汉的居住遗址。废弃的居住地，经过数千年的风化堆积，形成了灰黑色的土质。更令人吃惊的是，考古人员在兴隆沟遗址发掘出了碳化粟颗粒。这些谷物颗粒，是人工栽培形态的遗留物，距今已有 7700 年到 8000 年的历史。

On the vast open ground, a train of grey and black earth circles attracts the attention of students. These earth circles are the residence sites of Chinese ancestors in Aohan during the Neolithic Age about 8000 years ago. After thousands of years of weathering accumulation, abandoned residential areas have formed grey-black soils. More surprisingly, archaeologists unearthed grain of carbonized millet at the Xinglonggou site. These millet grains are the remnants of the artificial cultivation, which has a history of 7700 to 8000 years.

碳化粟 / Carbonized millet

河北省　武安市磁山博物馆内
In Cishan Museum, Wu'an City, Hebei Province

　　1972 年的冬天，武安磁山村的村民在开挖水渠时，意外发现了一座在地下沉睡已久的"原始村落"。经过文物部门对磁山文化遗址的发掘，发现了距今超过 8700 年的碳化粟。根据考古学家的推断，早在近万年以前，粟已经在磁山一带被广泛栽培。

In the winter of 1972, while digging ditches, the Cishan villagers in Wu' an City unexpectedly discovered a "primitive village" that had been sleeping underground for a long time. The carbonized millet grains over 8700 years have been found through the excavation of Cishan cultural site. Millet crops had been widely cultivated in Cishan area nearly ten thousand years ago according to archaeologists' inference.

事实上，中国粟的出土遗存多达五六十处，分布于河北省、陕西省、河南省、甘肃省、内蒙古自治区等十几个省（自治区），且大多集中在黄河流域。黄河流域，是中华文明的起源中心。为什么是粟成为中华先民栽培的首选？它是原产于中国，还是从境外传播而来？

In fact, as many as 50 ～ 60 remnants with millet grains were unearthed in China, distributed in more than a dozen provinces such as Hebei, Shaanxi, Henan, Gansu, Inner Mongolia, and mostly concentrated in the Yellow River Basin which is the origin center of Chinese civilization. Why is millet the first choice for cultivation of Chinese ancestors? Did it originate in China or was it introduced from abroad?

粟的起源 / The source of millet

刁现民 / 中国农业科学院研究员

Professor Diao Xianmin, Chinese Academy of Agricultural Sciences

刁现民是国家谷子产业体系首席专家，他在收集一种在敖汉旗随处可见的野生植物——狗尾草，这种在普通人眼中毫不起眼的杂草，刁现民却视若珍宝。

Diao Xianmin is the chief expert of the national millet industry system. He is collecting a wild plant that can be seen everywhere in Aohan Banner—— bristlegrass, a weed that is not noticeable in the eyes of ordinary people, but treasured by Diao Xianmin.

任何作物的起源，都是从这种原始的、野生的草来的，那么我们谷子的起源也是一样。从原来的狗尾草，

19

驯化到今天的谷子,经历了数千年,甚至上万年的变化。

Any crop is originated from wild grass, so is the foxtail millet. We have learned that their genes, or chromosomes, are almost the same through molecular biology and cytogenetics study. From the genomic level, it is proved that bristlegrass is the ancestor of foxtail millet.

刁现民 / *Diao Xianmin*

它不仅证实了谷子与狗尾草之间的亲缘关系,也确认了中国谷子的起源。我国栽培的谷子,并非由国外传入,而是由我国的青狗尾草经人工驯化而来。中华先民发现了狗尾草的天然变异现象,从中选择具有"穗大、不落粒、分蘖少"等对人类有利变异的个体,进行特殊培育,将这些优良性状稳定地传递下去。

It confirms not only the relationship between millet and bristlegrass, but also the origination of foxtail millet in China.

粟的驯化
The domestication of millet

The cultivated foxtail millet in our country is not introduced from abroad, but domesticated from the local Chinese green bristlegrass. Chinese ancestors discovered the natural variation of bristlegrass, and selected individuals with "big spike, no grain shattering, few tillers" which meet human needs, and carried out special means to transfer these elite traits steadily.

狗尾草 / Bristlegrass

谷子 / Millet

21

狗尾草和谷子有很大的区别。谷子植株高大、分蘖少、不落粒、籽粒大、香味多，从原来的狗尾草，驯化到今天的谷子，经历了数千年，甚至上万年的变化。它是一步一步地，变成不落粒，这个驯化过程由分蘖很多变为分蘖很少，实际上就是一个永远在驯化、永远在改良的过程。实现了从狗尾巴草到农家品种，再到今天栽培种的一个过程。

There is a big difference between bristlegrass and millet. Millet plants are tall, with fewer tillers, less grain shattering, big grains and more fragrance. The domestication from original bristlegrass to today's foxtail millet has undergone thousand years or more. The practice is step by step. The plant changed from grain shattering to non-shattering, from many tillers to few tillers. In fact, this is an endless process for domestication and improvement, which achieved the changes from bristlegrass to landraces and to cultivars today.

刁现民 / Diao Xianmin

结束了敖汉之行的刁现民，回到了北京的实验室。

这里保存着上千种狗尾草种子，它们来自全国各地，其中隐藏着与谷子亲缘关系最近的几个品种。

After Aohan's trip, Diao Xianmin returned to the laboratory in Beijing, where seeds from thousands of bristlegrass species are preserved. They came from all over the country, including some close relatives to foxtail millet.

我们不好说最早的谷子究竟从哪个点来的，但是可以肯定，它出自黄河流域是没有问题的。谷子在黄河流域首先被栽培，形成一个作物以后，就向四周扩散，扩散到中国的各个地方，以及世界其他国家。

It's hard to tell the exact point that the earliest millet came from. But surely it came from the Yellow River basin. Millet was first cultivated in the Yellow River Basin. After becoming a crop, it spread to all parts of China, then the world.

刁现民 / Diao Xianmin

中国的谷子，起源于黄河流域，这个观点在业内已经基本达成共识。粟被人工驯化之后，伴随着人们

的迁徙往来，从黄河流域逐渐向四外扩散开来。

China's millet is originated from the Yellow River Basin, which has been basically agreed in academics. After the domestication, along with people's migration, millet gradually spread out from the Yellow River Basin.

黄河 / Yellow River

在万年粟作中，自然灾害常常让农民面对歉收甚至绝收的困境。河北蔚县，始建于明永乐元年的常平仓，是中国古代官府为调节粮价、储粮备荒、供应官需民食而设置的粮仓。常平仓最早出现于2000多年前的战国时期，并被之后的王朝沿袭。直到今天，依然具有重要的意义。

In thousands of years of millet cultivation, farmers often face the predicament of poor or even no harvest under natural disasters. In Yuxian County, Hebei Province, Changping granary was built in the first year of Yongle in Ming Dynasty. It was a grain warehouse set up by the ancient Chinese government to regulate grain prices, store grain for scarcity, and supply food for the government and the people. Changping granary first appeared in the Warring States Period, 2000 years ago, and was inherited by later dynasties. To this day, it is still of great significance.

常平仓 / Changping granary

像常平仓这种伴随粟作而生的机制，几乎渗透于古代中国社会的每一个链条之中。粟的驯化，让中华民族步入一个全新的时代。

Such a mechanism as Changping granary, which was born with millet cultivation, permeated almost every chain of ancient Chinese society. The domestication of millet has brought the Chinese nation into a new era.

曹幸穗／中国农业博物馆　研究员
Professor Cao Xingsui, China Agricultural Museum

粟与人类文明
Millet and human civilization

粟驯化出来后，人类开始定居，有了剩余的粮食、剩余的资产，开始有社会初步的分工，农业开始产生。

26

人类从粟出现开始定居,定居以后开始有了社会分工,社会分工以后开始有了文明的积累,文明的积累就形成了我们后来的中华文明的源头。

After the domestication of millet, human beings began to settle down, and then they had surplus food and assets. They began to have a preliminary division of labor in society, agriculture began to emerge.Human beings began to settle down from the domestication. After that they began to have social division of labor, then the civilization was pushed and developed, which formed the source of Chinese civilization.

曹幸穗 / Cao Xingsui

兴隆沟遗址 / Xinglonggou site

27

这种社会分工的出现，对中国社会的演变具有划时代的意义。在社会分工的基础上，阶级分化、社会组织相继出现，最终形成了国家。至此，华夏先民告别了史前时代，进入了全新的文明时代——农业文明时代。而这一切，都与粟的驯化相伴相生。

The emergence of this social division of labor has epochal significance for the evolution of Chinese society. Based on social division of labor, class differentiation and social organizations emerged one after another, and finally the state was formed. At this point, the Chinese ancestors left the prehistoric era and entered a new era of civilization, that is the era of agricultural civilization. And all these are accompanied by the domestication of millet.

很长一段历史时期内，粟在中国古代的粮食作物中，占据着重要而特殊的地位。中华先民逐渐形成了以种粟为主，以采集、渔猎为辅的生活方式，并开始饲喂家猪、家狗、家鸡等畜禽。人类从渔猎采集时代，正向着一个新的时代迈进。

For a long period of time, millet occupied an important and special position in China's ancient grain crops. The

Chinese ancestors gradually formed a life style of planting millet, supplemented by collecting and hunting, and began feeding pigs, dogs, chickens and other livestock and poultry. Human beings moved from the era of fishing and hunting to a new era.

这些精美的文物，诞生于距今 5000 年左右的红山文化时期，当时，一部分人已经开始脱离农业生产，专门从事玉器雕刻、泥塑等工作。在粟的滋养下，文明有了质的飞跃，更加灿烂的文化因此孕育而生。

These exquisite cultural relics were born in the Hongshan culture period about 5000 years ago. At that time, some people began to deviate from agriculture and specialize in jade carving, clay sculpture and other works. Under the nourishment of millet, civilization has made a qualitative leap, and more splendid culture has been bred.

在河北武安磁山遗址，考古人员还发掘出碳化的榛果与核桃，以及石器、陶器、骨器等遗物 4000 余件。在这些遗物中，有用来为谷物脱皮的石磨盘、石磨棒，有用来做饭的泥制陶盂和支架及罐、钵、壶等容器，还有捕鱼用的骨镞，以及猪骨、鸡骨等禽畜骨骼的化石。

透过这些珍贵的文物，考古人员推断，伴随着粟的驯化，中华先民们结束了"逐水草而居"的游牧生活。

At the Cishan historical site in Wu'an City, Hebei Province, archaeologists also unearthed carbonized hazelnut and walnut, as well as more than 4000 of stone, pottery, bone and other relics. Among these relics, there are stone mills, stone grinding rods for grain peeling, clay pots and supports and containers such as pots, bowls and jars for cooking, as well as skeletons and fossils of animal and poultry bones such as pig bones and chicken bone for fishing. Through these precious cultural relics, archaeologists infer that with the domestication of millet, the Chinese ancestors ended their nomadic life of "living by river and grass".

陶罐 / Pots

猪骨 / Pig bones

石磨盘　石磨棒
Stone mill and stone grinding rod

伴随着粟作的发展，中国人制定了二十四节气，用来指导农事。在最基本的食物功能之外，粟还发挥着很多重要的职能。它充当了实物地租、实物货币和官员的俸禄。

With the development of millet cultivation, the ancient Chinese formulated 24 solar terms to guide farming. In addition to the most basic food function, millet also plays important roles. For instance, it acted as rent, currency and salary of officials.

粟的生产和储积，不仅关系到百姓生存，还深刻影响着国家的经济、政治安全，是统治者治国安邦之本务。正如战国时期著名的政治家商鞅所言："民不逃粟，野无荒草，则国富，国富者强。"

The production and storage of millet were not only related to people's livelihood, but also had profound impacts on economic and political security of the country. It was the fundamental task for the rulers to govern the country and to keep the country safe. As Shang Yang, a famous politician in the Warring States Period, said, "If the people do not evade millet (tax) and there is no wild grass in the field, the country will be rich and strong."

因为当时国家的经济、文化中心在淮河以北地区，我们 60% ~ 70% 的人口也是在淮河以北地区，可以说我们中华民族的祖先，大部分人是以小米为主粮的。粟，古代的时候也叫稷，我们叫社稷就代表国家，稷能够达到代表国家的程度，可见稷在这个国家的地位有多高。

At that time, the economic and cultural center of the country was in the north of the Huaihe River, covering 60% ~ 70% of the population. So most ancestors mainly ate millet. Millet is also called Ji in ancient times. Sheji in Chinese represents the nation. The Ji can reach the level of representing the nation, and shows the high position in the country.

曹幸穗 / Cao Xingsui

粟的辉煌一直延续到隋唐时期，中唐以后，黄河流域频发的战乱与自然灾害，让中原居民不断南迁。

Sui and Tang Dynasties witnessed the brilliance of millet. After the mid-Tang Dynasty, the frequent conflicts and natural disasters in the Yellow River Basin caused the residents of the Central Plains to move southward.

但是，迁移到南方的中原百姓，并没有继续种植谷子，而是和当地人一样，种起了另外一种重要的作

物——水稻。而在北方，4000 多年前由西亚传入我国的小麦，随着农业的发展及灌溉技术的进步，产量得到了明显的提升。更为重要的是，石磨技术的改进和普及，让粒食主导的古代中国，感受到了小麦磨制成面粉的美味。这种口感上的优势，让小麦的地位逐渐超过了粟。而属于谷子的荣光，仿佛在转瞬之间，便被人遗忘。

The people of the Central Plains who migrated to the South did not continue to grow millet, like the local people, they planted another important crop, rice. In the north, wheat was introduced into Ch ina from West Asia more than 4000 years ago. With the development of agriculture and the progress of irrigation technology, the yield has been significantly improved. More importantly, the improvement and popularization of stone milling let ancient Chinese who rely on grain food taste the delicacy of milled wheat flour. This advantage has made wheat more important than millet. And the glory of millet seems to be forgotten in an instant.

粟，从极致的绚烂，最终归于沉寂，在今天又逐渐发散出星火之光。她的前世，交织着我们往日的来路；她的今生，依旧可以给我们的未来新的启迪。而在未来，粟又将绽放出怎样的光彩？

Millet experiences the extreme gorgeousness and eventual silence. Today, it is gradually emitting sparks of light again. Its past intertwined with our past life, while its present can still give us enlightenment for the future. And what kinds of brilliance does it bloom in the future?

谷子 / Millet

一粒小米的故事

The story of a millet

II 粟 种

Episode 2
Seeds of Millet

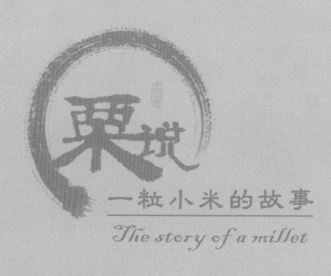

粟说

一粒小米的故事

The story of a millet

从古至今，中华民族对优良粟种的选择和培育，从根本上说，是从人的需求出发。它适应时代的发展，满足百姓更高层次、多个层次的需求，这是真正意义上的以人为本。

From ancient times to the present,the selection and breeding of elite millet seed fundamentally meet the human needs for Chinese nation. It adapts to the development of the times and meets the high and multiple levels of people's needs. This is people-oriented in the true sense.

刘旭/中国工程院　院士

Academician Liu Xu,Chinese Academy of Engineering

引 言 / Introduction

　　谷子花静静绽放，大美无声。清风徐来，花粉飘散，谷粒悄悄孕育。谷粒是等待收获的果实，也是来年播撒的种子。小小的粟种，决定着产量的高低、风味的优劣，以及颜色、形态的千变万化。

谷子花 / Millet flowers

Millet flowers blossom quietly, beautiful and silent. The breeze slowly comes, the pollen disperses, the grain quietly breeds. Grain is the fruit waiting to be harvested and the seed sown next year. Small millet seeds determine the yield, quality, and the ever-changing colors and shapes.

谷粒 / Millet grain

41

粟种里的文化密码
Cultural codes in millet

群山深处，陆平带领的考察队行色匆匆。他从1000多千米之外的北京，来到这个南方的山村，为的是收集一种作物的种子。

Deep in the mountains, Lu Ping led the expedition team in a hurry. They came to this southern mountain village from Beijing, more than 1000 km away, to collect millet seeds.

浙江省　杭州市建德市高丘村
Gaoqiu Village, Jiande City, Hangzhou City, Zhejiang Province

陆平1982年大学毕业，分配到中国农业科学院作物资源研究所。1996年以后转到谷子研究方面，对谷子进行专项的资源考察收集。在大多数人的印象中，江南是稻米之乡，很难和谷子联系到一起。事实上，不只是江南，在中国广大的南方地区，谷子是一种普遍而顽强的存在。

Lu Ping, graduated from university in 1982 and began to work at the Institute of Crop Resources, Chinese Academy of Agricultural Sciences. After 1996, he carried out millet research and collected germplasm of millet. Most people impressed that south of China is the hometown of rice, actually, millet is a common and tenacious existence in the vast southern region of China.

陆平 / 中国农业科学院　研究员

Professor Lu Ping, Chinese Academy of Agricultural Sciences

谷子起源于中国的黄河流域，伴随着百姓的迁徙，传播到中国各地。位于大山深处的高丘村，隐藏着陆平梦寐以求的农家品种。

Millet originated in the Yellow River Basin of China and

粟|说
The story of a millet
一粒小米的故事spread to all parts of country along with the migration of the people. Gaoqiu Village, deep in the mountains, hides the landraces that Lu Ping has always dreamed of.

谷子在广东省、广西壮族自治区、贵州省、云南省、四川省等地,都有很大面积的种植。老品种有很多优势,对当地的气候、环境、土壤适应性非常强,产量也很稳定,对以后新品种的改良是非常有用的。

There are large areas of millet planting in Guangdong Province, Guangxi Zhuang Autonomous Region, Guizhou Province, Yunnan Province and Sichuan Province. Landraces have many advantages, including strong adaptability to local climates, environments and soils. The yield is also stable. It is very useful for the improvement of new breed in the future.

陆 平 / Lu Ping

这里的谷子品种,被当地人称为黄粟,是一种糯性品种。黄壳白粒。出酒率高,每 100 千克谷子,可酿酒 40 ~ 50 千克。在陆平看来,一个品种的保存,不仅对于育种意义重大,也关系到一种文化的存留。

The landrace in this village, known as the yellow millet by the local people, is a waxy cultivar, with yellow shell and white grains. It can produce 40~50 kg of liquor per 100 kg of millet grain. In Lu Ping's view, the preservation of a landrace is not only significant for breeding, but also related to the preservation of a culture.

收集农家种 / Collect landraces

但在今天，谷子种质资源的收集与保护，也面临着严峻的挑战。

But today, the collection and protection of millet germplasm are also facing severe challenges.

这个黄粟抗病性非常好，穗子、长相都非常好，又不早衰。品种是与人文有关系的，品种保存下来，这种文化才能保存下来。尤其在农村，机械化程度越来越高，交通越来越方便，这些老品种往往丧失得非常快。

This yellow millet has excellent disease resistance. Its spike and appearance are very good, and there is no early senescence. Varieties are related to humanities. Only when varieties are preserved can this culture be preserved. Especially in the countryside, the mechanization level is getting higher and higher, and the transportation is becoming more and more convenient. Then these landraces are often lost very quickly.

陆　平 / Lu Ping

自 2015 年起，我国组织开展第三次全国农作物种质资源普查与收集行动。陆平和他的同事，几乎跑遍了全国各地。越是交通闭塞的地方，找到传统农家种的概率越大。

Since 2015, China has organized the third national survey and collection of crop germplasm resources. Lu Ping and his colleagues have traveled almost all over the country. The more difficult a place to reach, the more likely it is to find landraces.

收集农家种 / Collect landraces

国家作物种质库，是全国作物种质资源长期保存中心，各地收集来的谷种，都在这里进行保存。每个谷子品种保存 100 克，大约两三万粒，平均分成 3 份，送入贮藏区。

The National Crop Germplasm Bank is the national center for crop germplasm resources long-term preservation, where stores the seeds collected form nationwide. 100 grams seeds of each millet cultivar, about 20, 000 ～ 30, 000 grains, are divided into 3 equal parts and stored.

受一位育种家所托，陆平到这里帮忙寻找几份材料。贮藏区的温度常年恒定在 −18℃，种子在这里能够保存 50 年。

Lu Ping comes and helps a breeder to get some germplasm. The storage temperature is constant at −18℃ all year round. The seed can be kept for 50 years under this condition.

国家作物种质库里保存了 27000 个谷子品种。我们需要用的时候，随时拿出来用，这就是一种双重的财富：物质财富和精神财富。

27,000 millet varieties have been preserved in the National Crop Germplasm Bank. We can take it while in need. This is a kind of wealth, both material and spiritual.

陆　平 / Lu Ping

北京市　中国农业科学院国家作物种质库
National Crop Germplasm Bank of Chinese Academy of Agricultural
Sciences,Beijing City

粟种选育 / Millet breeding

　　相对于陆平收集种质资源的辛苦，一个品种的选育，更是来之不易，常常要经历漫长岁月的积累。粟是由野生狗尾草驯化而来，本身就是一种自然选择基础上的人工选择。自粟作诞生以来，这种选择从未停止。

Comparing with Lu Ping's hard work in collecting germplasm resources, the breeding is more difficult. It is time consuming to breed a new variety. Millet is domesticated from bristlegrass, which is an artificial selection based on natural selection. Since the birth of millet, this selection has never stopped.

　　成书于春秋时期的《诗经》中，便有了"粒选法"

《齐民要术》和《氾胜之书》
QiMin YaoShu and *Fansheng's book*

的相关文字；2000多年前，西汉晚期的重要农学著作《氾胜之书》中，则有了"穗选法"的相关记载。而在距今大约1500年的《齐民要术》中，记载了100多个作物品种，其中谷子品种就有86个，并记录了以穗选法为基础，从选种、留种到建立"种子田"的混合选种法。到了明清时期，我国又总结出了单株选择法，也叫"一株传""一穗传"。

Records of millet related words "grain selection method" were traced back to around 2000 years ago in the *Book of Songs* written during the Spring and Autumn Period. More than 2000 years ago, "panicle selection method" was recorded in an important agronomic work *Fansheng's book* during the

late Western Han Dynasty's period. In another book named *QiMin YaoShu* about 1500 years ago, more than 100 crop varieties were recorded, including 86 millet varieties. A mixed selection method based on panicle selection was recorded, explaining a program of seed selection, seed preservation and the establishment of seed production field. In the Ming and Qing Dynasties, a method of individual plant selection, also known as "single plant selection" and "single panicle selection", was summarized.

万年粟作中，选育出了丰富多样的谷子品种，它们遍布中国各地，呈现不同的形态与颜色。山西沁州黄小米、山东龙山小米、金乡金谷米、蔚县桃花米等优质名米，在时光的积淀中流传至今。

Millet varieties and landraces have been developed in cultivation for thousands of years and planted all over China, showing various shapes and colors. Qinzhou yellow millet, Longshan millet,Jinxiang golden millet,Yuxian peach-blossom millet and other famous millet landraces with high quality have been passed on to date.

形态各异的谷穗 / Various shapes of spikes

粟种改良 / Seed improvement

对风味与口感不断改良，为百姓培育出更好吃的小米，是从古至今，育种人不变的追求。十几年来，刘金荣一直专注于选育适宜煮粥的谷子品种。"豫谷18"，是刘金荣通过杂交技术，选育出的优良品种。

The continuous improvement of flavor and taste has been the constant pursuit of breeders since ancient times. For more than ten years, Liu Jinrong keeps focusing on breeding millet varieties for porridge cooking."Yugu 18"is an excellent variety developed by Liu Jinrong through hybridization.

刘金荣 / 河南省安阳市农业科学研究院　研究员
Professor Liu Jinrong, Anyang Academy of Agricultural Sciences, Henan Province

育种方向，第一个是谷子好吃，优质；第二个就是高产，抗倒、抗病。2009 年评优质米的时候，"豫谷 18"米的颜色和口感方面评分是最高的。

Taste and quality are the first current breeding target; high yielding, lodging tolerance and disease resistance are at the second position. In 2009 quality millet competition, the color and taste of "Yugu 18" scored the highest.

刘金荣 / Liu Jinrong

杂交育种，是通过人工手段，让不同的谷子品种通过杂交产生新品种。谷子是雌雄同花、自花授粉的作物，一朵谷子花中，既有雄蕊，又有雌蕊。杂交育种，需要剔除母本花雄蕊的花药，这个过程叫作人工去雄。用父本雄蕊的花粉，给母本雌蕊人工授粉，就完成了一次杂交的过程。

Hybrid breeding is to cross different millet cultivars to generate new cultivars through hybridization manually. Millet is a monoecious, self-pollinating plant. In a millet flower, there are both stamens and pistils. Hybrid breeding requires the removal of anthers from the female plant, which is called artificial emasculation. Artificial pollination of female plant pistils with the pollen of male plant completes a hybridization process.

为了赶上清晨 6 点左右的开花高峰，刘金荣每天清晨 4 点多起床，团队十几个人齐上阵，一天能做 30 来个杂交穗。

In order to catch up with the flowering peak around 6 o'clock in the morning, Liu Jinrong gets up at 4 o'clock every day. More than ten team members can make around 30 hybrid panicles a day.

杂交育种 / Crossbreeding

每天做不了几个穗。充其量也就三四个。必须经过大量试验、大量比较才能出东西，除了技术以外，有时要靠运气。

One person can only complete pollination for 3 to 4 panicles in a day. A lot of trails and comparisons are needed to achieve good results. Sometimes you have to be lucky besides technology.

刘金荣 / Liu Jinrong

种质资源创造
Germplasm creation

程汝宏 / 河北省农林科学研究院　研究员

Professor Cheng Ruhong, Hebei Academy of Agriculture and Forestry Sciences

　　程汝宏的百亩试验田里，要播下 17000 多份试验种。每年，他都要在这里进行大量的杂交试验。与刘金荣的育种方向不同，程汝宏更加关注谷子栽培模式的转变。

　　In Cheng Ruhong's 7 hectares experimental field, over 17,000 seeds will be sown. Every year, he conducts a mass of

57

hybridization experiments here. Different from Liu Jinrong's research field of breeding , Cheng Ruhong pays more attention to the transformation of cultivation patterns.

谷子是对除草剂非常敏感的一种作物，同时它是一种小粒作物。1000 粒种子只有 3 克，1 斤种子多达15 万到 18 万粒。生产中，我们有效的播种量只需要二三两，但实际工作中，在旱地上种植，种少了，保不住苗，种多了，需要人工间苗。长期以来，传统的谷子生产，一直依靠人工除草、人工间苗。

Millet is a small grain crop extremely sensitive to herbicide. 1000 seeds weigh 3 g, and 0.5 kg seads contains 150,000 to 180,000 grains. In production, the theoretical effective seeding rate is 100 to 150 g, but in practice, on non-irrigated land, if we seed less, it cannot get enough seedlings, if we seed excessively, it needs artificial seedlings thinning. For a long time, traditional millet production has relied on artificial weeding and seedling thinning.

程汝宏 / Cheng Ruhong

程汝宏用栽培谷子与青狗尾草抗除草剂突变体进行远缘杂交。

Cheng Ruhong made hybridization of cultivated millet and bristlegrass herbicide-resistant mutant.

"冀谷39",是由3个同型姊妹系组成的,类似于3胞胎。1个是抗2种除草剂的双抗品系,1个是抗1种除草剂的单抗品系,还有一个不抗除草剂的品系。我们在应用中,可以两两组合,形成双胞胎系,也可以3个一块组合形成3胞胎系。出苗以后,根据苗多苗少情况,我们可以灵活间苗。苗比较多的情况下,我们可以杀掉不抗除草剂的系和单抗除草剂的系,如果苗比较合适,多一点点的情况下,我们可以杀掉一

个系。我们用的除草剂，都是高效低毒的除草剂，它的残效期只有 40 天左右。

"Jigu 39" is composed of three siblings of the same type, similar to triplets, a dual-resistance strain to two herbicides, a monoclonal-resistance strain to one herbicide, and a non-herbicide-resistant strain. In application, we can make combination of each two strains to form twin strains, or triplet. After seedling emergence, according to the quantity of seedlings, we can flexibly thinning by getting rid of non-herbicide resistant lines and monoclonal herbicide resistant lines. The herbicides we use are all highly effective and low toxic. The residual period is only about 40 days.

程汝宏 / Cheng Ruhong

程汝宏试验田的这几畦谷子，具有高油酸性状，种子来自国家作物种质库。

These plots of millet in Cheng Ruhong's experimental field have high oleic acid properties. The seeds came from the National Crop Germplasm Bank.

程汝宏要利用这些谷子做母本，选育出具有高油酸性状的新品种，用于小米深加工产品的生产。

Cheng Ruhong will use these germplasms as female parents to breed new cultivars with high oleic acid content for fine processing.

这些是从陆平那 2 万多份材料里找出来的，已经搁了十几年了，没人用。油酸含量低，容易导致谷子加工食品在运输、储藏、销售过程中的酸败，对人体是有害的。

They were selected from more than 20,000 landraces with the help of Lu Ping. They have been laid aside for over ten years. Low oleic acid content can easily lead the processed millet food to go rancid during the transportation, storage and marketing, which is harmful to go human.

程汝宏 / Cheng Ruhong

通过杂交，培育高油酸的品种，能够延长小米的保质期，满足加工的需要。

Through hybridization, high oleic acid varieties can prolong shelf life of millet products and meet the needs of processing.

温汤杀雄 / Warm water sterilization

这种人工去雄的方法，叫作温汤杀雄，利用的是雄蕊和雌蕊对相同温度的不同反应。用47℃温水去雄，能够将花粉杀掉，而保持雌蕊也就是柱头不受伤害。

This method of artificial emasculation is called warm water sterilization, which utilizes the different sensitivities of stamens and pistils to temperature by 47 degrees of warm water for castration. When pollen is killed, the pistil, or stigma, is unharmed.

完成了授粉工作，程汝宏在高油酸分离群体中采集了一些谷子叶，匆匆赶回实验室。一项重要的工作正等待着他。

After completing pollination work, Cheng Ruhong

collected some millet leaves from the high oleic acid separation group and rushed back to the laboratory. An important job is waiting for him.

　　程汝宏在寻找控制高油酸的基因。谷子有 9 条染色体，上万个基因。找到这个关键基因，会让之后的育种事半功倍。密码，就隐藏在谷子的叶片里。

Cheng Ruhong is looking for genes that control high oleic acid trait. Millet has nine chromosomes and tens of thousands of genes. Finding this key gene will make the breeding work more efficient. The secret is behind in the leaves.

基因测序 / Gene sequencing

　　每一个性状，都是由相应的基因来控制的，我们找到控制的基因，就可以通过室内检测，确定哪一株含有这个基因，那么我们的育种效率，可以成百倍地提高。通过找到高油酸的基因，来培育高油酸的谷子品种，延长谷子的保质期，将来用我们的谷子加工的食品，能够被人们大量食用，我们可以以更多的形式，来消费高营养的小米食品。

　　Each trait is controlled by the corresponding gene. Once the controlling gene is identified, we can determine which plant contains the gene through indoor testing. Then the breeding efficiency can be improved hundreds of times. By finding genes controlling high oleic acid content, new variety with high oleic acid would be developed to prolong shelf life of millet. In the future, people will eat and consume more processed millet foods that contain much nutrients.

程汝宏 / Cheng Ruhong

　　通过对后代基因型的分析和选择，来选育新的品种，代表着育种领域最先进的方向，也推动着谷子种质资源创新的步伐。适合糖尿病患者食用的"冀谷

T7"等品种先后选育成功，这些新品种的出现，拓展了谷子的用途，满足了百姓更高层次的需求。

To breed new varieties through the analysis and selection of offspring genotypes represents the most advanced direction in breeding, and also drives the pace of innovation of millet germplasm resources. "Jigu T7" and other varieties that suitable for diabetic patients have been successfully developed. The emergence of these new varieties has expanded the use of millet and satisfied the high level needs of the people.

将来我们还可以培育更多用途的谷子品种，比如富含维生素 E 的品种、富含赖氨酸的品种等。

In the future, we can develop more varieties of millet, such as those rich in vitamin E, lysine and so on.

程汝宏 / Cheng Ruhong

抗除草剂谷子
Herbicide-resistant millet

40 千米之外，聂志德的谷子种植基地，已经感受到"冀谷 39"带来的巨大改变。2012 年，经商多年的老聂，成立了谷子合作社。3000 亩谷子地，全部播完只需要一周左右。而十几天后的间苗环节，将充分发挥出"冀谷 39"的优势。

Forty kilometers away, Nie Zhide's millet planting base has experienced the tremendous changes brought by "Jigu 39". In 2012, Nie, who had been in business for many years, established a millet cooperative. It only takes about a week to sow all the 200 hectares of millet land. Ten days later, at the seedling-thinning stage, "Jigu 39" will play its full advantages.

谷子播种 / Sowing millet seeds

聂志德 / Nie Zhide

间苗最重要的是掌握时机，一般在谷子长到 3 个叶的时候就开始间苗。人工间苗太费劳力了，一般一个青壮劳力，一天间不了一亩地。

The most important thing for seedling thinning is to grasp the opportunity. Generally, it begins when millet grows to three leaves. Artificial thinning is especially labour consuming. In general, a young man can only thin no more than 700m^2 in a day.

聂志德 / Nie Zhide

与谷苗一起疯长的，还有各种杂草。间苗、除草要同步进行。否则，谷苗很快就会被生命力更加旺盛的杂草淹没。

Many kinds of weeds grow with the millet seedlings. Thinning and weeding should be carried out simultaneously. Otherwise, the seedlings will soon be submerged by the vigorous weeds.

不抗除草剂的死掉了，抗除草剂的留下了，这就起到了间苗的作用。一亩地基本上保证在 35000 ~ 40000 棵这样。现在咱用自走式喷药机，一天能完成二三百亩的作业。

The non-herbicide resistant plant is dead while the herbicide resistant plant is viable. In this way the seedling thinning is fulfilled. 35,000 to 40,000 seedlings are basically guaranteed in 700m^2 field. Now we use self-propelled spraying machine to complete 15 to 20 hectares field in a day.

聂志德 / Nie Zhide

间苗的同时，田间的杂草被消灭掉了，效率得到了明显的提升。品种的改良，使谷子生产实现了机械化的大跨越，这种划时代的改变，对于老聂已经习以为常。

At the same time of thinning, weeds in the field were also eliminated, and the efficiency was obviously improved. The improvement of cultivars has made millet production realize mechanization, which is a great progress. This huge change has become common to Nie.

使用除草剂间苗 / Use herbicide for thinning out

喷药后第六天，不抗除草剂的谷子苗，以及田间的杂草都开始枯萎。这样的结果，老聂很满意。

Six days after spraying, non-herbicide resistant millet seedlings and weeds in the field began to wither. Nie is satisfied with the result.

400 千米之外的张家口，已经到了谷子授粉的时节。产量低，曾经是制约谷子产业发展的瓶颈。赵治海对于杂交谷子的研究，改写了谷子产量低的历史。

It is time for millet pollination in Zhangjiakou, 400 kilometers away from Nie. Low output was once the bottleneck restricting the development of millet industry. Zhao Zhihai's research on hybrid millet has rewritten the history of low yield.

赵治海 / 张家口农业科学研究院　研究员

Professor Zhao Zhihai, Zhang Jiakou Academy of Agricultural Sciences, Hebei Province

我们按照科学方法选出亲本来，一个母本一个父本，它具备了不同的两种遗传背景，杂交以后会焕发出更强大的生长势和生长力，这就是杂交种的优势的

杂交谷子
Hybrid of millet

表现。

We select parents with different genetic backgrounds. Hybrids would show heterosis of strong growth potential and power.

赵治海 / Zhao Zhihai

谷子花粉弥散 / Pollen diffusion

无人机授粉 / Unmanned aerial vehicle pollination

利用无人机旋翼的风力，为谷子进行授粉，将大大提高授粉的效率。

Using the wind power of unmanned aerial vehicle to conduct pollination will greatly improve the efficiency.

人工授粉要耗费大量的人力，而且授粉有一个时间限制，一般就是在半个小时之内，它要完成这个授粉的工作，一个人也就走个两三亩，但是无人机可以迅速在50亩谷子地的上面盘旋完成这个过程，授粉效果也好，成本也低。

Artificial pollination is labor intensive. Furthermore, there is a 30 minutes limitation for pollination. Within 30 minutes, one person can complete 1500~2000m^2 of field work. UVA 3.3 hectares of millet land, with better pollination effect and lower cost.

赵治海 / Zhao Zhihai

杂交种制种田 / Hybrid farming

　　这些谷子，在高度上有明显的区别。高的是父本，矮的谷子，为光温敏型雄性不育系，这种谷子的谷穗，雄蕊不能产生有功能的花粉，但它的雌蕊发育正常，能接受正常花粉受精结实。利用这种谷子作为杂交中的母本，大规模的杂交制种得以开展，杂种优势得到了充分的利用。

　　These millets are obviously different in height. The male plant is much taller. The shorter one is the photothermo-sensitive male sterile line, which cannot produce functional pollens. But its pistils develop normally and can accept normal pollen fertilization and fruiting. Utilizing this millet as the female plant in crossing, we may produce largescale of hybrid seeds, and the heterosis could fully performed.

73

从 2000 年到 2017 年，赵治海先后选育出张杂谷系列十几个品种。张家口地区谷子亩产从原来的二三百斤，增加到 800 斤以上。

From 2000 to 2017, Zhao Zhihai had developed a dozen varieties of "Zhangzagu" series. In Zhangjiakou City, the millet output increased from 1.5 tons to over 6 tons per hectare.

杂交谷子大田生产 / Hybrid of millet field

杂交，才能够有优势。同样的种子，杂交以后，同样的水、肥、光照、土壤，产量会增加很多。还是那块地，但是产量增产二三百斤，就给老百姓能多增收二三百斤的效益。

Hybridization could produce heterosis. Hybrids yield

much more under the same condition of water, fertilizer, light and soil. The output increased 100 to 150 kilograms on the same piece of land, farmers would benefit more from the increasing.

赵治海 / Zhao Zhihai

杂交谷的出现，改写了我国春播旱地谷子产量低的历史；已经走出国门，在埃塞俄比亚、纳米比亚、尼日利亚、乌干达、赞比亚等非洲国家生根发芽。

The appearance of hybrid has rewritten the low yielding history of spring-sown dryland millet in China. The hybrid millet has gone abroad and widely applied in Ethiopia, Namibia, Nigeria, Uganda, Zambia and other African countries.

杂交试验 / Breeding experiment

10月，赵治海的试验田，迎来了又一个丰收。程汝宏抗除草剂谷子也大面积丰收。

In October, Zhao Zhihai's experimental field ushered in another bumper harvest, the same as for Cheng Ruhong's large area of herbicide-resistant millet.

从古至今，粟种的不断改良，带来口味的提升和产量的增加，以及用途的不断扩展，成就栽培方式的蜕变，地膜覆盖精量播种正在逐渐推广开来。覆膜、播种、施肥、铺设滴灌管，一次性完成，省去了后期间苗环节。古老的作物，今天依然焕发勃勃生机。

Since ancient times, the continuous improvement of millet has brought the promotion of taste and yield, as well as the continuous expansion of application, which has resulted in the progress of cultivation methods. Precision seeding with plastic film mulching is gradually popularized. Completing film mulching, seeding, fertilization and laying drip irrigation pipe in one time, can eliminate the stage of thinning. Millet, this ancient crop, catches up the pace of modernization.

马天进／贵州省农林科学研究院　研究员

Professor Ma Tianjin, Guizhou Academy of Agriculture and Forestry Sciences

　　育种人的终极理想，与几千年前的中华先祖并无二致——选育出更加适宜的品种，满足百姓更高层次的需求。以不断的继承、创新与更迭，来应对世界的变化——这是粟种的秘密，也是中华民族生生不息的秘密。

The ultimate ideal of breeders is the same as that of Chinese ancestors thousands of years ago that is developing perfect varieties to meet people's higher needs. Coping with the ever-changing world through continuous succession, innovation and alternation is not only the secret of millet, but also the secret of the endless life of Chinese nation.

粟说
一粒小米的故事
The story of a millet

III 粟味

Episode 3
Flavor of Millet

粟说

一粒小米的故事

The story of a millet

中国人在饮食上，讲究"食不厌精脍不厌细"，这折射着中华民族对生活品质的追求。而在新的时代，对品质更深层次的追求，就是对健康更大的追求。粟本身的营养价值，就决定了它在健康中国大背景下的不可或缺。

Chinese people are particular about fine and delicate foods, which reflects the pursuit of life quality. In the new era, striving for quality is the demand of becoming healthier. Millet's nutritive value determines its indispensable position under the background of healthy China.

刘旭／中国工程院　院士
Academician Liu Xu,Chinese Academy of Engineering

引 言 / Introduction

有一种食物的味道，与我们相伴万年。

她，是朴素的清香。

她，是变换的美味。

她改变着我们，也被我们改变。

小米虾排 / Millet shrimp row

82

The story of a millet
一立小米的故事

A taste of food has been with us for ten thousands of years.

It is a simple scent.

It is the ever changing delicacy.

It influences people's food style.

小米挂面 / Millet noddles

吉林　吉林市龙潭区乌拉街
Wula Street, Jilin City, Jilin Province

松花江 / The Songhua River

　　白露刚过，渐浓的秋味笼罩着松花江畔的乌拉街。乌拉是满语，意思为沿江。早晨9点多钟，露水渐消。

Just after Bailu (Bailu is one of the twenty-four solar terms, and it is between September 7—9 each year), the scent of autumn gradually covered the Wula Street along the

Songhua River. Nine o'clock in the morning, the dew gradually
disappears.

眼下正是谷子成熟后期,还有十几天就能收获。
常恕清要到 2000 米外的谷子地里看看。2016 年接受
新型职业农民培训后,常恕清开始走订单种植的路子。

It's the late ripening stage and millet will be harvested in
about ten days. Chang Shuqing wants to check the millet field
2km away. Chang began to grow millet according to orders
after the training on the new type professional farmers in 2016.

常恕清 / Chang Shuqing

乌拉街小米,在清朝时,全部逐级进贡,一直献
到皇宫。曾经高高在上的贡米,如今已经走进寻常百
姓家。

85

Wula Street millet, in the Qing Dynasty, was all paid as tribute to the imperial palace. Once the high-class millet has now entered the ordinary homes.

乌拉白小米 / Wula white millet

小米的营养 / Nutrition of millet

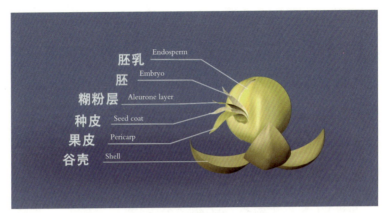

胚乳　Endosperm
胚　Embryo
糊粉层　Aleurone layer
种皮　Seed coat
果皮　Pericarp
谷壳　Shell

小米的营养成分 / The nutritional content of millet

　　小米是谷子的产物。谷子由谷壳、果皮、种皮、糊粉层、胚和胚乳组成，脱去谷壳剩余的部分就是糙米。糙米去掉果皮、种皮，糊粉层和胚，剩下的胚乳才是精米，就是我们餐桌上常见的小米。

Millet grain consists of shell, pericarp, seed coat, aleurone layer, embryo and endosperm. The remaining part, off the shell, is brown millet. After removing the pericarp , seed coat, aleurone layer and embryo, the brown millet becomes polished millet, which is the common millet on our table.

　　小米富含蛋白质、脂肪和碳水化合物，以及人体必需的维生素、矿物质和膳食纤维。中华先民驯化出了谷子，从此便拥有了营养全面而均衡的小米。

Millet is rich in protein, fat and carbohydrates, as well as essential vitamins, minerals and dietary fiber. The Chinese ancestors domesticated the millet crop and obtained the millet with comprehensive and balanced nutrition.

在涉县这样的谷子主产区，小米饭是从古至今最为重要的主食。而在今天中国广大的北方地区，更具代表性的小米食物是小米粥。小米粥不仅常常出现在北方人日常的三餐之中，还是妇女分娩后重要的进补食物。小米粥易消化吸收，并极大限度地保留了小米中的营养精华。丰富的 B 族维生素，以及铁、钾、镁等矿物质，得到了更为充分的利用。

In the main millet producing areas like Shexian, millet is the most important staple food since ancient times. In today's vast northern region of China, the more representative millet food is millet porridge. Millet porridge is not only often in the daily three meals of northerners, but also an important supplementary food for women after childbirth. Millet porridge is easy to digest and it is one of the best ways to retain the nutrient components of millet. Rich B vitamins, iron, potassium, magnesium and other minerals in millet have been fully utilized.

河北省　涉县王金庄旱作梯田

Terraced fields of dryland farming in Wangjinzhuang, She County, Hebei Province

吃小米饭 / Eat millet rice

89

马志敏 / 石家庄市妇产医院围产中心　主任
Ma Zhimin, Director of Perinatal Center, Shijiazhuang Obstetrics and
Gynecology Hospital

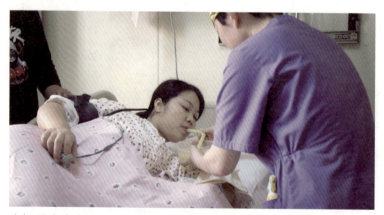

产妇喝小米粥 / Puerpera has millet porridge

　　产妇产后第一餐就可以进食小米，其中维生素 B1
位于我们粮食之首。B 族维生素对神经系统调理具有
非常重要的作用，所以对产后恢复精力是非常有好处

的。小米因为含有铁、钾、镁这些矿物质，所以对缺血性贫血的一些产妇也是非常有意义的。另外，小米含有大量的膳食纤维，所以对便秘的产妇是非常有好处的。

We can eat millet at the first meal after delivery, of which vitamin B1 is the richest among all cereals. B vitamins are very important for nervous system conditioning. It's very good for postpartum recovery. In addition, millet contains minerals of iron, potassium and magnesium minerals, so it is very helpful for those pregnant women with ischemic anemia. Moreover, dietary fiber in millet is very good for constipated parturient.

马志敏 / Ma Zhimin

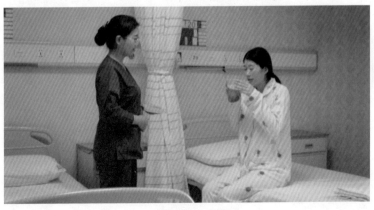

产妇喝小米粥 / Puerpera has millet porridge

小米粥 / Millet porridge

小米油 / Top layer of the porridge

代参汤
Substitute for ginseng decoction

小米熬成粥后，很大一部分营养进入米汤中，特别是浮在最上面一层的米油，是米汤的精华，有"代参汤"之美誉。

Millet congee contains a large part of the nutrition, especially the millet oil on the top layer is the cream of the porridge and has the reputation of "substitute for ginseng decoction".

小米油可以作为婴幼儿的补充辅助食物，最初可以单纯用点小米油，用点小米汤，也就是平常熬的，慢慢可以加一些菜叶，甚至有的拿小米油冲一些奶粉都是可以的。

Millet oil can be used as an important supplementary food for infants. At first, millet oil can be eaten directly. Along with the infant growth, vegetable leaves can be added and even formula can be dissolved in millet oil.

马志敏 / Ma Zhimin

餐桌上的小米
Millet on the table

The story of a millet

在与小米相伴的漫长岁月中，祖国医学早已发现了小米在养生、保健方面的作用。

In the long run of companion with millet, traditional Chinese medicine practitioners have already discovered the function of millet in health preservation and health care.

李佃贵 / 国医大师

Li Diangui， Master of Chinese physician

　　小米的作用，一个是补先天，一个是补后天，先天是补肾，后天就是健脾。因为中医说脾为后天之本，肾为先天之本，所以先天和后天之本都可以补得充足了。像矿难的病人啊，增加他的体力是非常重要的。

　　The function of millet is to supplement congenital and acquired for vital energy and blood, digestion and sleeping. For instance, the first meal for survivals from mine accident is usually millet porridge, which can increase their physical strength.

李佃贵 / Li Diangui

随着中国人在烹饪方法上的不断探索，小米粥也开始呈现不同的姿态与风味。海参，与小米结合，具有很高的营养价值，味道更是咸鲜醇香，回味无穷。

With the continuous exploration of Chinese cooking methods, millet porridge also began to show different postures and flavors. Sea cucumber, combined with millet, has a high nutritional value. The taste is delicious and mellow, leading a person to endless aftertaste.

小米是一个食药两用的东西。海参更是食药两用的，它是补肾的。小米有健脾作用，又有补肾作用，所以两者的功能是相似的，小米和海参合在一起吃有补肾健脾、养生的作用。

Millet and sea cucumber are health foods both for edible and medical use. They have common functions of invigorating vital energy and digestion. Eating millet with sea cucumber can enhance the health care function.

李佃贵 / Li Diangui

对于中国人而言，食物的美味，与营养价值同样

重要。人们不断探索新的烹饪方式，创造出更加丰富的味觉体验。

For Chinese, food delicacy is as important as nutritional value. People are constantly exploring new cooking methods to create a richer taste experience.

小米海参粥 / Sea cucumber and millet porridge

2002 年，考古人员在青海省喇家遗址发现了 4000 年前的面条。面条完好地保存在一个倒扣的碗中，出土时显示为纯正的米黄色，这碗面条的原料是粟和黍，这是目前所知的世界上最早的面条。

In 2002, archaeologists discovered noodles made 4000 years ago at Lajia site in Qinghai Province. The noodles were well preserved in an inverted bowl when unearthed as pure beige. The noodles were made from millets, regarded as the earliest noodles in the world.

青海省　海东市民和回族土族自治县喇家遗址
Lajia Site in Minhe Hui and Tu Autonomous County, Haidong City ,
Qinghai Province

世界上最早的面条 / The earliest noodle in the world

形态的改变，让小米不再局限于传统的粒食方式，中国人开始了新的味觉探索之旅。

With the change of forms, millet is no longer limited to the traditional way of grain eating. Chinese people have begun a new journey of taste exploration.

手抓小米饭 / Millet rice

油炸果子 / Fried millet ball

98

河北省沧州市泊头市交河镇，一座北方小镇，因当地非常流行吃交河煎饼，素有"南京到北京，走到交河吃煎饼"的说法。因为轮班，常年北漂的李晓玉，终于可以跟家人一起过个团圆的元宵节。

Jiaohe Town, Botou City, Cangzhou City in Hebei Province, a small town in the north, is very popular for Jiaohe pancakes. It is known as "From Nanjing to Beijing, go to Jiaohe to eat pancakes". Li Xiaoyu, a Beijing Drifter, can finally have the Lantern Festival of reunion with her family between shifts.

母亲教李晓玉摊煎饼
Her mother taught Li Xiaoyu how to make pancakes

交河煎饼至今已有 300 多年的历史，其主料为小米和绿豆。绿豆中的赖氨酸，弥补了小米中赖氨酸的不足，使营养更加均衡。交河煎饼的做法来源于山东

99

煎饼。山东煎饼形似荷叶，薄软如纸，卷上大葱、其他蔬菜、肉类，就是山东人从小吃到大的舌尖美味。

Jiaohe pancake has a history of more than 300 years. Its main ingredients are millet and mung beans. Mung bean makes up for the deficiency of lysine in millet and makes nutrition more balanced. Jiaohe pancake comes from Shandong pancake. Shandong pancake looks like a lotus leaf, soft as paper, rolled with scallions, other vegetables and meat. It is the tasty delicacies of Shandong people from the young to the old.

山东煎饼 / Shandong pancake

据说，当年一户姓张的人家，从山东迁到现在的交河西关。为了生计，他们开始制作煎饼出售。初期，张家煎饼跟老家山东的煎饼一样，后来，他们根据当地人的口味，在煎饼中间放入菜馅，逐渐形成了"交河煎饼"。

It is said that a family surnamed Zhang moved from Shandong to the current Jiaohe. To make a living, they began to make and sell pancakes. At the beginning, Zhang's pancake was the same as those in Shandong Province. Later, according to the local taste, they put vegetable fillings inside pancakes. Gradually this kind of pancake became the famous "Jiaohe pancake".

交河煎饼 / Jiaohe pancake

晓玉家，母亲连夜赶制煎饼，为的是让在异乡打拼的女儿，能带上一份故乡的记忆。离别如期而至，新的一年即将开始。这是世界上最珍贵的舌尖美味。带着妈妈的味道，前路的孤单也变得温暖。

At Xiaoyu's home, her mother is making pancakes, which carry the memory of hometown. Xiaoyu will take the memory and be back to her work ing place. The departure time is coming, and a new year is about to begin. This is the most precious delicacy for Xiaoyu. Surrounded by mom's love, she feels warm and not alone on her life journey.

晓玉离家打工 / Xiaoyu leaves home for working

百年南和煎饼
Nanhe pancake for hundreds of years

赵国强 / 南和煎饼第四代传承人
Zhao Guoqiang, the fourth generation successor of Nanhe pancake

在相距 200 多千米的河北省邢台市南和区，煎饼成为别样的存在。赵国强，南和煎饼第四代传承人，祖传的南和煎饼传承至今已经有百余年的历史。赵国强对其进行了现代化的创新。

200 km south to Jiaohe, in Nanhe County, Hebei Province, pancake becomes another kind of existence. Zhao Guoqiang is the fourth generation successor of Nanhe pancake. The pancake has a history of over 100 years. Zhao Guoqiang makes innovations.

比如说，我们加了核桃，另外，加了葡萄干，再一个，加了芝麻，从创新的角度讲，也是为了膳食营养更均衡。

For example, we add walnuts, raisins, and sesame. It is also for a more balanced diet from an innovative point of view.

赵国强 / Zhao Guoqiang

南和煎饼 / Nanhe pancake

香糯小米糍粑
Sweet glutinous millet cake

贵州省　黄平县谷陇镇
Gulong Town, Huangping County, Guizhou Province

谷子收获 / Corn harvest

　　在黄平县东部的谷陇镇，98% 的居民是苗族人。谷陇镇山清水秀，成片的稻田随处可见。而在山坡和山顶上的零星旱地里，种植着一种南方并不多见的作物——谷子。当地种植的是一种叫作大白谷的传统品种，这种小米糯性好、品质佳，对于当地以稻作为主

105

的苗家人来说，显得尤为珍贵。

In Gulong Town, east of Huangping County, 98% of the inhabitants are Hmong. Paddy fields can be seen everywhere. On the slopes and top of the hills, there is a rare crop in the south, that is millet. A traditional variety called Great White Millet is grown locally. This kind of millet has good glutinous property and good quality. It is especially precious for the locals whose main crop is rice.

在太平村，准备回娘家的苗族姑娘张晒海，正忙着制作小米糍粑。在苗寨，小米被视为最有营养的食物。小米淘洗干净，浸泡一晚。把淘好的小米放入木甑中蒸制。蒸制，是人类改变小米形态、构建人类餐桌文化的早期烹饪方式。两个小时后，将蒸熟的小米，从甑中挖出来，趁热放入木臼中。

In Taiping Village, Zhang Shaihai, a Hmong girl, who is going back to her mother's home, is busy making steamed millet cakes. In Hmong village, millet is regarded as the most nutritious food. Washed, soaked overnight, steamed in a wooden steamer for two hours, the millet is transferred to wooden mortar while it was hot. Steaming, an early cooking way to change the form of millet, belongs to a part of human

table culture.

张晒海淘米 / Zhang Shaihai is washing the millet

木甑蒸小米 / Steamed in wooden steamer

　　打糍粑是个体力活。张晒海请来邻居帮忙，边打边揉。小米的糯性被激发出来，手心沾上一层化开的猪油，掐出一块，揉成圆饼，凉置一夜。在竹篓的四角，

装饰上染红的鸭蛋。张晒海踏上了回娘家的路。

Making steamed millet cakes is a kind of physical work. Zhang asks her neighbor for help. Kneading and beating stimulate the glutinous nature of millet. Covered with a layer of melted lard on hands, a piece of dough is pinched out and

打糍粑 / Making steamed millet cake

糍粑 / Steamed millet cake

kneaded into a round cake. Keep the cakes cool over night and
place into the bamboo basket decorated with colored duck
eggs at four corners. Zhang sets foot on her way back to her
mother's home.

挂上彩色的鸭蛋 / Decorated with colored duck eggs

大白谷制成的小米糍粑，是张晒海这样的出嫁女儿回娘家时，带给母亲的最好礼物。

The steamed millet cake made from Great White Millet is the best gift for a married daughter like Zhang Shaihai when she returns to her mother's home.

一家人吃小米糍粑 / Family get together to eat steamed millet cake

烤糍粑 / Bake steamed millet cake

等级最高待客之礼
The highest level of hospitality

苗寨 / Hmong Village

苗族老人 / Old women of Hmong

在黄平的苗寨人家，还隐藏着另外一道以小米和猪肉为主材，蒸制而成的佳肴。在贵州，食用小米鲊，已有数百年的历史。

In Huangping's Hmong family, there is another steamed dish with millet and pork as the main ingredients. In Guizhou Province, "mizha" has been eaten for hundreds of years.

The story of a millet 一位小米的故事

111

准备长桌宴 / Preparing long table banquet

小米鲊 / Mizha

老一辈苗家妇女认为，制作小米鲊是女娃们从小就必须学会的技能。糯米绵密弹牙，牵牵连连间肉香扑面而来。在当地，小米鲊被奉为等级最高的待客之礼。这样的长桌宴可以持续到第二天天亮。

The older generation of Hmong women believe that

making "mizha" is a skill that girls have to master. The glutinous millet is soft and elastic, mixing with meat smell. In local, the "mizha" is regarded as the highest level of hospitality for guests. Such a long table banquet can last until the next day.

长桌宴 / Long table banquet

从烹饪方式的不断丰富，到自身形态的改变，从主食，到大菜，再到小食，小米呈现着不同的姿态和风味。中国人赋予小米更为微妙的变化，调剂着百姓每一个寻常日子。

From the continuous enrich cooking methods to the change of forms, from staple food to dishes and snacks, millet presents different postures and flavors. The Chinese people have given millet diversified changes, which enrichs the daily life.

The story of a millet

一 粒 小 米 的 故 事

冻米糖 / Hard millet candy

小米牛肉丸 / Beaf ball with millet

小米锅巴 / Millet rice crust

114

油炸小米虾排 / Fried millet shrimp steak

小米炒面 / Millet Fried flour

红谷酿醋
Red valley vinegar

　　时间的艺术，总会给食物蒙上一层神秘的面纱，揭开面纱的那一刻，转化的灵感便在不经意间显现出来。李猛，王村醋第六代传承人。每天，他跟二舅牛海均学习古老的酿醋技法。牛海均是王村醋第五代传

115

承人，在自己的酿醋作坊干了大半辈子。李猛原本在
市里的一家医药公司做销售，2014 年，李猛决定回到
家乡，将二舅的老手艺延续下去。

The time always covers a mysterious veil on food. When
the veil is lifted, the inspiration of transformation will appear
inadvertently. Li Meng, the sixth generation successor of
Wangcun vinegar. Every day, Li learns the old vinegar-making
techniques from his uncle Niu Haijun. Niu is the fifth generation
successor of Wangcun vinegar and spends most of his life
in his vinegar-making workshop. Li originally worked for a
pharmaceutical company in downtown.In 2014, he decided to go
back to his hometown and inherits his uncle's traditional skills.

山东省　淄博市周村区王村镇　李猛
Li Meng，Wangcun Town, Zhoucun District, Zibo City, Shandong Province

数千年前，我们的祖先就已掌握谷物制醋的技术。王村醋，是以当地的红谷小米为主要原料进行酿造的。李猛决定在传承古法的基础上进行创新。他专门走访了山东省农业科学院和淄博市农业科学研究院的相关专家，对他自己种植的红谷进行提纯。经过近3年的努力，传统酿醋技艺在李猛的手里重焕生机。

Thousands of years ago, Chinese ancestors had mastered the technology of making vinegar from grain. Wangcun vinegar is brewed with local red millet as the main raw material. Li decided to innovate on the basis of the ancient process. He consulted experts of Shandong Academy of Agricultural Sciences and Zibo Agricultural Sciences Research Institute to purify the red millet variety which he planted. With three years of efforts, the traditional vinegar-making skills rejuvenated by Li Meng.

山东省　淄博市周村区王村镇　李猛
Li Meng，Wangcun Town，Zhoucun District,Zibo City，
Shandong Province

小米醋 / Millet vinegar

古法制黄酒
The ancient method of making millet wine

一个开门声，唤醒了在酒坛中沉睡十年之久的珍贵黄酒。原本经营白酒生意的赵生满，嗅到了黄酒经营的商机，转身开始酿造小米黄酒。但黄酒酿造工艺因年代久远，早已失传，想要恢复并非易事。

Opening the door, it shows the precious millet wine that had been stored in the jar for ten years. Zhao Shengman, who was originally engaged in liquor business, sniffed the business opportunity of millet wine and turned to start brewing. However, it is not easy because the brewing knowhow of millet wine has been lost for a long time.

河北省　张家口市怀来县　赵生满
Zhao Shengman, Huailai County,Zhangjiakou City,Hebei Province

泡米两天，发酵四五天，压榨又一天，全是这样的。

119

一笼下来就是十八天。坏了就再重来，找原因。

Two days for soaking, 4 to 5 days for fermentation, and a day for press, the whole circle will cost 18 days. If it's not succeed, another circle will be needed again and again to find the reason.

赵生满 / Zhao Shengman

发酵 / Fermentation

赵生满足足用了一年的时间，借助残缺不全的古方，终于按照古法酿制成传统的黄酒。人生一世，交错着日常的三餐和一场场筵席，小米醋和小米黄酒，便是粟在时光的转化中，诠释出的人间滋味。

It took Zhao a full year to successfully make traditional millet wine with the help of fragmentary ancient methods.

Three daily meals and feasts involve in one's life. Millet vinegar and wine, as the passengers of millet, interpret the taste of life as time going by.

河北省　张家口市怀来县　赵生满
Zhao Shengman, Huailai county,Zhangjiakou City，Hebei Province

小米黄酒 / Millet wine

小米走向深加工

Further processing of millet

小米营养粉生产线 / Millet nutrition powder production line

小米馒头 / Millet steam bread

　　为了更充分地发挥小米在健康方面的作用，小米深加工产业，正受到越来越多科研人员的重视。我国谷子主要分布在河北省、山西省、内蒙古自治区、吉林省、陕西省等北方省（自治区），小米深加工产品也主要分布在这些区域。

　　In order to play full role of health function, an increasing

122

number of researchers are paying attention to millet deep processing industry. Millet in China is mainly distributed in Hebei, Shanxi, Inner Mongolia, Jilin, Shaanxi and other northern provinces, the deep-processing products are also mainly distributed in these areas.

李顺国 / 河北省农林科学院　研究员
Professor Li Shunguo, Hebei Academy of Agriculture and Forestry Sciences

小米碗粥 / Millet porridge

　　小米深加工产品，像小米营养粉，主要分布在山西省及安徽省等一些地区；小米煎饼主要分布在山东省，一些小米煎饼已经形成主食工业化的水平；还有小米醋，主要分布在河北省、山西省、山东省等地。

The deep processed products such as millet powder is mainly distributed in Shanxi Province, Anhui Province and other regions. Millet pancakes are mainly distributed in Shandong Province, and some have industrialized as staple food. Vinegar is mainly distributed in Hebei, Shanxi and Shandong provinces.

李顺国 / Li Shunguo

　　时至今日，一些传统的小米产品，已经可以通过现代化的生产技术，实现主食工业化，同时，加工更多的方便食品，适应现代人快节奏的消费需求也正在成为现实。

Today, some traditional millet products can industrialize staple food through modern technology. At the same time, processing more instant foods to meet the fast-paced consumption needs of modern people is also becoming a reality.

　　在加工小米面条方面，因为小米本身不含面筋蛋白，可以通过现代技术改变小米的加工特性，如通过添加小麦强筋粉，改善小米面条的口感，来加工小米面条。随着人们健康、保健意识的增强，对小米的消费需求也越来越多。全国的谷子生产面积在逐年扩大，一些地方已经从谷子主产区，向谷子产业区转变，最终向谷子聚集区转变；一些地方已经建设各具特色的一、二、三产业融合发展的谷子产业园区。

Because millet itself does not contain gluten protein, through adding wheat gluten powder to improve the taste of millet noodles, we can easily make millet noodles. With the enhancement of people's health awareness, the demand for millet consumption is also increasing. The area of millet production in China is expanding year by year. Some places have transferred from the main millet producing area to millet industrial area, and finally to the millet industry cluster area. Some places have built millet industrial parks with different characteristics of integration of primary, secondary and tertiary sectors.

李顺国 / Li Shunguo

小米与健康
Millet and health

沈群教授正在研发更多的小米深加工产品，挖掘小米在现代社会中的新价值。研发新的深加工产品的同时，沈群教授带领的团队，开展了小米功能特性的研究，并有了重要的发现。

Professor Shen Qun is developing more deep-processed millet products to explore the new value of millet in modern society. Besides of developing new deep-processed products, Professor Shen Qun's team also carries out research on the functional characteristics of millet and has made a lot of progress.

沈群 / 中国农业大学　教授
Professor Shen Qun, China Agricultural University

主要是来改善小米的风味、口感，能够提高它的连食性，能够天天吃，所以，在这个方面，我们主要是做出更好吃的小米和其他杂粮的一些食品。

We have been improving the flavor and taste of millet, so that it can be eaten every day. At this respect, we mainly make some better millet foods.

沈群 / Shen Qun

小米营养成分的挖掘和现代化生产，给现代人快节奏的生活建立起一种天然的保护屏障，为现代人的餐桌提供多样化的健康味道。

The study on millet nutrients and production modernization have established a natural health barrier for modern people's fast-paced lifestyle and provided diversified healthy tastes on dining tables.

我们现在逐步地认识到小米有很多的功能特性，比如，它能降血糖、降血脂、降血压，还有助眠等作用。通过小米的膳食干预，对糖耐量减低人群的血糖控制有非常明显的效果。未来小米加工产品会越来越多，而且会越来越好吃。

The story of a millet
一 粒 小 米 的 故 事

We are gradually recognizing that millet has many special functions, such as regulating blood sugar, blood pressure, blood lipid, and helping to sleep. Through the dietary intervention of millet, it is effective for diabetics to control the blood sugar. In the future, more and more millet products will appear with better flavor.

沈群 / Shen Qun

沈群 / 中国农业大学　教授
Professor Shen Qun, China Agricultural University

作为大米、小麦之外的重要补充，小米重新占据中国人的餐桌，将以另一种姿态，改良中国人的饮食版图，为建设健康中国，发挥出自己的一分力量。粟的味道，是近万年前哺育华夏先民的淡淡的甜，是食

128

不厌精、脍不厌细的浓郁的香，更是契合于中国人身体与基因深处的健康之味。

As an important supplement to rice and wheat, millet reoccupys Chinese dining table and will improve the dietary structure and play its part in building a healthy China. Millet, nourishing Chinese for thousands of years, tastes light sweet and mellow fragrant. It has integrated into the inner Chinese.

小米牛肉粒 / Millet rice with fried beef

一粒小米的故事

The story of a millet

IV 粟 魂

Episode 4
Soul of Millet

粟说

一粒小米的故事

The story of a millet

一方面，谷子坚韧、抗逆，从不向恶劣的自然环境低头；另一方面，它是一种环境友好型作物，与自然维系着天然的平衡，一面是抗争、奋进，一面是宽和、仁厚；这是谷子的魂，也是中华民族之魂。

Millet is tough and stress resistant, never bow to harsh natural environment. However, it is an environmentally friendly crop, maintaining a natural balance with nature. On the one hand, it struggles and forges ahead; on the other hand, it is generous and kind. This is not only the soul of millet, but also the soul of the Chinese nation.

刘旭/中国工程院　院士

Academician Liu Xu,Chinese Academy of Engineering

引 言 / Introduction

　　谷子坚韧、抗逆，从不向恶劣的自然环境低头；另一方面，它是一种环境友好型作物，与自然维系着天然的平衡。一面是抗争、奋进；一面是宽和、仁厚；这是谷子的魂，也是中华民族之魂。

河北省　张家口市涿鹿县　民族柱

National stanchion, Zhuolu Country, Zhangjiakou City，Hebei Province

Millet is tough and stress resistant, never bow to harsh natural environment. However, it is an environmentally friendly crop, maintaining a natural balance with nature. On the one hand, it struggles and forges ahead; on the other hand, it is generous and kind. This is not only the soul of millet, but also the soul of the Chinese nation.

谷穗 / Millet spike

The story of a millet

《说文解字》 / *ShuoWen JieZi*

年与禾 / "Nian" and "he"

　　过年，是中国人最重要的习俗。甲骨文"年"字，上面为"禾"，下面为"人"，是"一个人背负着成熟谷子"的形象。东汉许慎编著的《说文解字》中有这样的解释："年，谷熟也"。意为：谷子成熟一次，便是一年。做年夜饭时，是每一个中国家庭最温馨祥和的时刻。

　　Spring Festival is the most important festival of Chinese. The oracle "nian" is formed by "he" on the top and "ren" at the bottom. It is the image of "a man carrying mature millet". In *ShuoWen JieZi*, compiled by Xu Shen in the Eastern Han Dynasty, there was such an explanation:"Nian, millet ripens", means millet ripens once represents a year. At

Lunar New Year's Eve dinner, every Chinese family will enjoy the most warm and peaceful moment.

河北省　涿鹿县 / Zhuolu Country, Hebei Province

侯站毅一家吃年夜饭
Hou's family is having New Year's Eve dinner

　　对于涿鹿人而言，大年夜一定要煮上一锅接年饭，是用当地产的小米，加上土豆熬制而成。三十晚上吃一部分，再留一部分，寓意年年有余。

Zhuolu people must cook a pot of food with millet and potatoes on New Year's Eve. At New Year's Eve, eating a part and leaving a part, implies every year have enough food to eat.

正月初一，侯站毅一家一大早便出了门。每年的这一天，涿鹿人都有一个重要的仪式。

On lunar January first, Hou's family went out early in the morning. Every year on this day, Zhuolu people have an important ceremony.

在《史记》记载中，大约五千年前，黄帝、炎帝所带领的部落，与蚩尤带领的部落，发生了涿鹿之战。最终，黄、炎部落赢得了战争的胜利，周围部落纷纷归顺，开启了中华民族大融合的先河。

In the *Records of History*, the tribes led by Emperor Huang and Yan fought against the tribe led by Chiyou in Zhuolu about five thousand years ago. Eventually, the Huang and Yan tribes won the victory of the war and the tribes nearby paid allegiance to them, pioneering the great integration of the Chinese nation.

重要的仪式 / Important ceremony

合符坛 / Unification Altar

千百年来，涿鹿当地人逐渐形成了一个固定的仪式，即在每年的正月初一，祭拜黄帝、炎帝和蚩尤。

For thousands of years, the local people of Zhuolu gradually formed a fixed ceremony. On the first day of every lunar January, they worship Emperors Huang, Yan and Chiyou.

三祖堂 / Three ancestor's hall

　　这个拜三祖，是继承的传统。老一辈儿去拜，到了我们小一辈儿也去拜，就是祈求来年风调雨顺、五谷丰登。

This worship is traditionally inherited. All the people from old generation to young generation would worship to pray for favorable weather and a bumper harvest year.

侯站毅 / Hou Zhanyi

拜三祖 / Ancestor worship

拜三祖 / Ancestor worship

燎疳
Jumping over the fire

The story of a millet
一立小米的故事

　　柴湘隆的一天，是从打水开始的。由于少雨和严重的水土流失，甘肃省会宁县成为中国最为缺水的地区之一。只有谷子等极少数作物，能够在这里生长。

　　Fetching water is the first job for Chai Xianglong in a day. With less rainfall and severe soil erosion, Huining County, Gansu Province, has become one of the most water-deficient areas in China. Only a few crops, such as millet could barely grow here.

　　柴家湾只有400多口人。从1977年恢复高考以来，先后走出了160多名大学生。贫瘠恶劣的环境，并没

能阻挡这里的人们向阳而生，奋力奔跑。他们有着和谷子一样冲破逆境的坚韧与顽强。

There are only more than 400 people in Chaijiawan and more than 160 students have been sent off since 1977. The barren and harsh environment does not stop people from pursuing the bright future. They are tough and persistent, just like millet.

甘肃省　会宁县柴家湾 / Chaijiawan,Huining County,Gansu Province

村民商量活动方案 / Old brothers gathered for activity plan

一大早，柴湘隆家就热闹了起来。几个老哥们聚到一起，为的是村子里一年一度的大事。

Early in the morning, the Chai family became exciting. Several old friends gathered at his home for the village's annual event.

一切商量妥当，柴湘隆和几个老哥们便赶往举办活动的涝坝。

When all were settled, Chai and several old friends rushed to the dam where the event would be held.

活动之前，准备好最为重要的物件——谷草。

Before the event, the most important thing ── millet grass, have to be prepared.

谷草 / Millet grass

涝坝里一片欢腾。晚上九点，柴湘隆点燃了谷草。

It is full of joy. At nine o'clock in the evening, Chai lights the millet grass.

点燃谷草 / Lights the millet grass

人都聚集到一起，准备五堆火，中间的是最大的，就是属于篝火形式，另外的小火是让人跳着过去的。跳火是为了祛百病，图个吉利。

Let's all get together and prepare five heaps of fire. The biggest one is in the middle, like campfire, other fours are prepared for people to jump over. Jumping fire is to dispel all kinds of diseases and make a good fortune.

柴湘隆 / Chai Xianglong

燎疳 / Jumping over the fire

燎疳 / Jumping over the fire

这种古老的传统，叫作燎疳，俗称翘火堆、跳火，是广泛流传于西北地区的春节习俗。当地有"正月二十三，家家户户都燎疳"的民谚。

This traditional event, commonly known as warping the heap of fire or jumping the fire, is a Spring Festival custom

widely spread in Northwest China. There is a local folk proverb, "On the twenty-third day of the first month of the lunar year, every household participate in fire jumping".

谷子因其顽强的抗逆性，在古老的年俗中扮演着举足轻重的角色。中华民族崇尚这种逆境中的抗争精神，因为这种精神，也流淌在中国人的血脉中。

Millet plays an important role in the ancient customs because of its tenacious resistance. The Chinese nation advocates the struggling spirit, which flows through the blood of Chinese people.

1936年10月，中国工农红军第一、第二、第四方面军在会宁会师，宣告着长征的胜利结束。

In October 1936, the First, Second and Fourth fronts of the Red Army joined forces in Huining and declared the victory of the Long March.

小米加步枪
Millet plus rifle

甘肃省 会宁县红军长征会师旧址

The old site of the Red Army joining force in the Long March in Huining Country, Gansu Province

甘肃省 会宁县红军长征会师旧址

The old site of the Red Army joining force in the Long March in Huining Country, Gansu Province

当年，会宁人民支援红军的物资之中，就有当地出产的小米，靠着这些重要的补给，经过短暂修整的红军再次踏上了革命的征途。

At that time, locally produced millet was supplementary

materials contributed by farmers for the Red Army. Relying on these important supplies, the Red Army, once again embarked on the revolutionary journey after a short period of renovation.

宝塔山 / Baota Mountain

延安革命纪念馆 / Yan'an Revolution Memorial

　　远在 600 千米之外的延安革命纪念馆，历史的画面依然清晰可见。1937 年，中共中央进驻延安，延安成为中国人民抗日战争的重要根据地。

600 km away, the Yan'an Revolution Memorial Hall presents an alive picture of history. In 1937, the Central Committee of the Communist Party of China stationed in Yan'an, which became an important base for the Chinese people's War of Resistance Against Japanese Aggression.

小米加步枪 / Millet plus rifle

1946 年 8 月,毛泽东在延安杨家岭会见美国记者安娜·路易斯·斯特朗时,曾特别强调:"我们所依靠的不过是小米加步枪,但是历史最后将证明,这小米加步枪比蒋介石的飞机加坦克还要强些。"

In August 1946, when Chairman Mao Zedong met with Anna Louis Strong, an American journalist in Yangjialing,

151

Yan'an, he stressed in particular, "We rely on millet plus rifles, but history will finally prove that this millet plus rifle is stronger than Chiang Kai—shek's aircraft plus tanks."

对于延安时期，小米加步枪的这段革命历史，单文纯老人有着深刻的记忆。

As for the revolutionary history of millet plus rifle in Yan'an period, Shan Wenchun has a deep memory.

单文纯　原 63 军 189 师政治部　副主任
Shan Wenchun, an old soldier

在武器落后的情况下，敌我双方实力悬殊，战士们靠着誓死保卫领土的抗争精神，在战场上奋勇杀敌。小米作为珍贵的军粮，支援着前线的战士。

Although we owned backward weapons and a wide difference between ourselves and the enemy, our soldiers fought

152

bravely relying on the spirit of defending the territory to the death. As a precious military food, millet supports the soldiers in the front line.

奋勇杀敌 / In battlefields

我们当时吃的就是老百姓供给部队的小米，根本吃不上什么小米干饭。我们一个班就一盆饭，班长只能给每个人分一小碗。那么一小碗饭，哪能吃饱啊，根本吃不饱。

What we eat at that time is millet supplied by people to the army. It is not enough. You know, we shared a pot of millet, everyone will take a small bowl, so small, how can we have enough to eat? We are not eating enough at all.

单文纯 / Shan Wenchun

在毛泽东"自己动手，丰衣足食"的号召下，边区军民大力开展农业生产，种植谷子等作物。

Under Mao Zedong's call of "do it ourself, get plenty of food and clothes", the military and civilians in the border areas vigorously carried out agricultural production and planted millet and other crops.

靠着小米和从敌人手中缴获的武器，我们的战士用坚韧和血泪，刻下中国民族革命史诗中铿锵有力的一笔。

Relying on millet and the weapons seized from the enemy, our soldiers carved a powerful stroke in the Chinese national revolutionary epic with tenacity and their lives.

冲锋陷阵 / Fight bravely

也就是那时，谷子身上的抗逆性，与红色精神的抗争性合二为一，成为激励身处艰难时世的中国人的精神图腾。

Exactly at that time, the stress resistance of millet integrated with the revolutionary spirit became a spiritual totem to inspire the Chinese people in difficult times.

米薪制
Rice salary system

鲜为人知的是，中华人民共和国成立初期，小米还曾经扮演过一个特殊的角色。这段尘封的历史，对于刘善祥和刘涌波两位老人来说，是一段难以忘怀的记忆。

Rarely known, millet also played a special role in the early days of the People's Republic of China foundation. It is an unforgettable memory for Liu Shanxiang and Liu Yongbo.

1949 年春，中华人民共和国成立前夕，当时还在晋察冀边区学习的刘涌波，与 30 多名同学一起，被派到刚刚解放的察哈尔省①的张家口。刘涌波被分配到当时的察哈尔省宣化县，正是在这里，她遇到了相守一生的伴侣——刘善祥。

In the spring of 1949, on the eve of the founding of the
① 察哈尔省，中国旧时省份，1952 年撤销。
① Chahar province, China's former province, abolished in 1952.

People's Repubic of China, Liu Yongbo, who was still studying in the Border Region Shanxi-Chahar-Hebei Provinces , was sent to Zhangjiakou, the capital city of Chahar Province, together with more than 30 students. Liu was assigned to Xuanhua County at that time. It was here where she met Liu Shanxiang, her lifelong companion.

刘善祥　河北省委原常委　省纪委原书记
刘涌波　河北省张家口市原经贸委　顾问
Liu Shanxiang, retired officer
Liu Yongbo, Liu Shanxiang's husband

　　两人因工作而相遇相知，如今已携手走过60多年。两位老人都已年近九旬，但依旧清晰地记得当年的工作点滴。

They met because of their work, and they have been together for more than sixty years. Both of them are nearly ninety years old, they still remember their routine work clearly.

刘善祥和刘涌波年轻时照片

The picture of young Liu Shanxiang and Liu Yongbo

　　中华人民共和国成立伊始，货币还未统一，物价不稳。小米不仅是充饥的粮食，在北方很多地区，还肩负着一项重要的职能，充当等价物。工人、教师的薪金以小米衡定，称为"米薪制"。而像刘善祥和刘涌波这样的干部，衣、食等生活必需品由国家供给，每个月的零用费，同样是以小米为标准制定。

　　At the beginning of the founding of the Pople' s Repubic of China, currencies were not unified and prices were unstable. Millet was not only food, but also serving as an equivalent in many areas of the north. The salaries of workers and teachers were paid by millet, which was called "millet salary system".

For cadres like Liu Shanxiang and Liu Yongbo, necessities such as clothing and food were provided by the state, and the monthly allowance was also based on millet.

米票 / Food stamps

每个月给4千克小米的钱，为什么是小米啊，那时物价不稳定。买点牙刷，买点牙粉，买个肥皂，买个碱面。肥皂也就是咱们的高档化妆品，肥皂就用来洗脸和洗衣服，洗头就用碱面。4千克小米就干这个，但是我们还有富余。

Anyway, we were given 4kg of millet a month. Why millet? The price then was not stable. To buy toothbrushes, toothpowder, soap and soda. Soap was our top-grade cosmetics and used to wash face and do the laundry , while we use soda to wash hair. 4kg of millet were used to buy these, but we still had surplus.

刘涌波 / *Liu Yongbo*

刘善祥和刘涌波早餐是小米粥
The breakfast is millet porridge

虽年至耄耋，但刘善祥和刘涌波两位老人，对于 4 千克小米零用钱的年代，依然记忆犹新！

Even though in their 90s, they still remember the days of 4 kg millet as allowance.

无论世事如何艰难，也不会改变内心的自洽与乐观。中国人有谷子一样的顽强坚韧，因而在面对逆境时，便多了几分笃定与从容。

No matter how difficult the life is, it will not change the inner self-consistency and optimism. The Chinese, as tenacity as millet, are more determined and calm while facing the adversity.

郭法曾与何玲正在给学生上课
Guo Fazeng and He Ling are giving lecture

谷子精神 / Spirit of millet

郭法曾，国家一级演员，也是一名优秀的导演。几年前，他和妻子何玲被聘任为邢台学院表演系的教师。

Guo Fazeng, an excellent director, is also a national first-class actor. A few years ago, he and his wife He Ling were appointed as teachers of the Department of Performance of Xingtai University.

在历史上，谷子对中华民族是立了大功的。其他农作物比如遇到天灾，有的地方就歉收，甚至有的地方就颗粒无收。这种情况下谷子照样还可以生存，还可以打粮食，所以在很多地方人们没有被饿死。它养育了我们中华民族一代又一代的人。

In history, millet has made great contributions to the Chinese nation. Other crops, in natural hazards, harvest little or nothing in some places. In this case, millet can still survive and harvest. So people are not starved to death because of millet. It has nurtured our Chinese people from generation to generation.

郭法曾 / Guo Fazeng

20 多年前，因为执导电视剧《李东辉》，原本对谷子一知半解的郭法曾，一步一步走近了这种作物。

More than 20 years ago, Guo Fazeng, who originally knew little about millet, stepped closer to the crop because he directed the TV drama *Li Donghui*.

1990 年 11 月，我国著名的谷子专家李东辉因肺癌去世。几年后，他的感人事迹，被郭法曾搬上荧屏，

诠释了谷子人身上的坚韧与执着。

In November 1990, Li Donghui, a famous millet expert in China, died of lung cancer. A few years later, his touching story was brought to the screen by Guo Fazeng, which explained the tenacity and persistence of millet scientists.

电视剧《李东辉》 / TV drama *Li Donghui*

谷子是在恶劣的情况下也能生长的一种农作物，李东辉在当时的农业科学研究上，没有那么多经费，在这样的环境下也可以从事谷子研究，说明他本身就有谷子精神。

Millet is such a crop that can grow in harsh conditions. Li Donghui did not have much funding for research at that time, but he persisted to conduct millet research under such circumstances. He had the spirit of millet.

郭法曾 / Guo Fazeng

电视剧《李东辉》/ TV drama *Li Donghui*

在患癌的 7 年时间里，李东辉怀着对谷子研究事业的满腔热血，争分夺秒，与病魔抗争，与时间赛跑，为后人留下了宝贵的科研成果，这是谷子人身上最真挚的谷子精神，这是谷子精神最生动的人格写照。

Suffering from cancer for 7 years, Li Donghui, fighting against the disease and racing against the time, left valuable achievements for future generations with his passion. This is the most sincere millet spirit in millet Scientists, which is the most vivid personality portrayal of millet spirit.

李东辉是专门研究谷子的，科研就是为生产服务的。后来就以这棵野生谷子为种，培育出了冀谷系列。

Li Donghui is specialized in millet research, scientific research is to serve the production. Later,"Jigu" series have been developed and cultivated from this wild millet.

电视剧《李东辉》台词 / Actor's lines of *Li Donghui*

郭法曾 / Guo Fazeng

在拍摄过程中，郭法曾和摄制组人员，也仿佛接受了一场精神洗礼，切身感受到谷子坚韧不屈的生命之魂，与中华民族血脉深处的精神共鸣。

During the shooting process, Guo Fazeng and the film

crew seemed to receive a spiritual baptism. They were touched by the soul of millet's tenacious life and the deep spiritual resonance of the Chinese nation.

它像奶水一样，像一位母亲一样，养育着中华民族，所以在我们这个《李东辉》电视剧的主题歌里，就有这样的歌词，"小米是奶，小米是娘，小米养活了儿女一双，一个叫黄河，一个叫长江"。

Like milk, like a mother, millet raises the Chinese nation. So, in the theme song of *Li Donghui* TV drama, there are such lyrics: millet is milk, millet is mother, millet feeds up a pair of children, one is the Yellow River, the other is the Yangtze River.

郭法曾 / Guo Fazeng

如今，郭法曾和爱人何玲把红色题材剧目带进校园，继续传承顽强不屈的谷子精神。

Nowadays, Guo Fazeng and his wife He Ling brought the red drama into the campus and passed through the indomitable spirit of millet.

中华民族其实是一个多灾多难的民族。但中华民族没倒，不但没倒，还发展成我们今天这个强大的民族，我们正向着更高的目标在前进，我们说谷子精神其实就是这种精神。

The Chinese nation is in fact a disaster-prone nation. But the Chinese nation has not collapsed, not only has it not collapsed, but also developed into a powerful nation today. We are making great progress encouraged by millet spirit.

郭法曾 / Guo Fazeng

而在谷子坚韧的外表之下，还有另一种为很多人所忽视的特质。在其发源的黄河流域，谷子于农历二月开始生长，八月成熟，处四季之中，得阴阳之和，古人因此称其为"禾"。在他们的观念中，禾是人类调和自然诸因素的产物。在与干旱、瘠薄环境的对抗中，谷子以其节水、省肥的特性，反过来又呵护着天地自然。

和为贵

Harmony is the most prized

Under the tough appearance of millet, there is another trait that many people ignore. In the Yellow River basin where it originated, millet begins to grow in March and ripen in September. It is in the best time of four seasons, it balances the Yin and Yang. The ancients therefore called it "he", the similar pronunciation of "harmony" in chinese . In their view, "he" is the harmony between human and nature. Millet, with less water and fertilizer demands, in turn to protect the nature, when confronting with drought and barren.

成熟的谷子 / Mature millet

一面是坚韧不屈，一面是温和宽厚，谷子的这种特质，与中华民族的精神属性，与崇尚"和为贵"的中华文化，产生了更深层次的共鸣。

Millet's characters, persistence and inclusiveness, have a deep resonance with the spiritual attributes of the Chinese nation and the Chinese culture which advocates "harmony is precious".

尹素哲 / Yin Suzhe

尹素哲，国画画家。最近，一位美术馆馆长向她求画，拟名《粟》。尹素哲一有空就琢磨。

Yin Suzhe is a Chinese painter. Recently, a curator of an art gallery asked her for a painting *Millet*.

于家石头村，距今已有 500 多年的历史。听闻这里有大片的谷子地，尹素哲立刻赶来。

和合而生
Arise in harmony and proper conditions

Yujia Stone Village has a history of more than 500 years. Yin Suzhe came here immediately when she heard that there was a large area of millet land in this village.

作画 / Painting

清风阵阵，谷穗低垂摇曳，叶子刚劲挺拔，谷子地里生发出天人合一的天籁之美。尹素哲找到了画中缺失的情感味道。灵感裹挟着情感瞬间倾泻而出，这时的她与谷子产生了深层共鸣。

The breeze blows, millet spikes are bent and swaying, leaves are straight, and the millet fields create the beauty of unity of nature and man. Yin Suzhe found the missed emotion in the painting. Inspiration suddenly appeared from her mind, and then she had a deep resonance with millet.

国画《粟》/ Traditional painting *Millet*

　　它长得是非常有特点的，就像一个个紧握的拳头一样，紧紧地挤在一起，好像攒着一股劲儿，有一种凝聚的力量。它虽然在贫瘠恶劣的环境中，但是依然能结出丰盈的谷穗。同时，谷子身上所维系着的和合而生的自然法则，不也正是和我们中华民族历来崇尚的天人合一思想不谋而合吗？

　　It is unique, like a clenched fist, tightly hold, as if there is a strength, a cohesive force. Although grow in poor and harsh environment, it can still produce rich grain spikes. At the same time, the natural law of harmony in millet coincides with the thought of unity between nature and man that the Chinese nation has always advocated.

尹素哲 / Yin Suzhe

因为饱含着对历史的记录，孕育着对未来的希冀，于是谷子那种富有生命力的和谐之美，就通过谷穗的饱满和叶片的锋韧传递出来。

Carrying the record of history and the hope for the future, millet's vitality of harmonious beauty is transmitted through the plump spikes and the tough leaves.

寄蜉蝣于天地　渺沧海之一粟
A mayfly between the sky and earth is like a grain of millet in the sea

一粒小米的故事
The story of a millet

黄土高原 / Loess plateau

粟，从农耕时代的起点一路走来，虽然渺小，却哺育出伟大的华夏文明；虽然低调，但也曾居庙堂之

高，成就江山社稷。穿越万年的时光，粟的角色也在转换更迭，但无论沧海桑田，粟还将和我们相依相伴。这是一粒小米的故事，也是中华民族的故事。

Millet, coming all the way from the beginning of the agrarian age, although small, has nurtured a great Chinese civilization; although modesty, once stands at high position and symbolized the nation. Throughout the thousands of years, the role of millet keeps changing. No matter how nature evolves, millet would accompany us in the future. This is a story about millet, also a story about Chinese nation.

谷穗 / Millet spike

谷穗 / Millet spike

龙图腾 / The dragon totem

The story of a millet
一 粒 小 米 的 故 事

骆占军 / Luo Zhanjun

导演札记
Notes from the Directors

　　创作历程，是对粟由浅入深的认知过程，也是内心被洗涤的过程。粟赋予了宁静，也赋予了力量！

　　The creation process is the cognition process of millet from shallow to deep, and also the process of soul being washed. Millet gives not only tranquility, but also strength.

粟 说
一 粒 小 米 的 故 事
The story of a millet

叶 明 / Ye Ming

小米的故事，是一个关乎选择的故事。

被发现，被拣选，被尊为五谷之首，成就江山社稷。

被取代，被冷落，被重新定义，助力健康中国。

是我们选择了小米，还是小米选择了我们？

岁月的年轮刻画了无数兴衰沉浮，

在历史浩瀚的烟波中，每个人都是沧海一粟。

Millet's story is a story of choice. Being found, chosen, and respected as the head of the grain, it creates the achievements of the country. Being replaced, left out, and redefined, it helps Chinese be healthy. Did we choose millet, or did it choose us? The rings of time have marked many ups and downs, everyone is a drop in the ocean of history.

焦　洁 / Jiao Jie

　　农耕文明的起点，创造了人类与粟的邂逅。而我
与粟的熟识，是因为遇到林林总总与粟相关的"人"和
"故事"。俯下身，去聆听，我祈望自己能够对每个个
体的喜怒哀乐感同身受。我眼中"他们的故事"变成了
"我们的故事"。在小米的生命传奇中，我们都是参与
者。坚韧执着的民族性格，是我们身上共同的烙印。

　　The starting point of farming civilization created the
encounter between human beings and millet. My acquaintance
with millet is due to the numerous "people" and "stories"
related to it. Bending down and listening, I wish I could feel
the pleasure, anger, sorrow, joy of each individual. In my eyes,
"their story" becomes "our story". We are all participants of
the millet's life legend. National characters of toughness and
persistence are our common imprint.

导演札记

Notes from the Directors

殷成杰 / Yin Chengjie

　　将近两年的时间，我用镜头不断记录春种、夏管、秋收、冬藏。我敬畏每一个干旱缺水的地区、每一位朴实厚道的农民、每一粒承载生命之重的小米。百代过客，中国人与小米，有着切割不断的血脉相连。不断记录故事，也是在记录信仰。

　　For nearly two years, I used the lens to continuously record the spring planting, the summer field management, the autumn harvest and the winter storage. I am in awe of every dry region, every simple and honest peasant, every grain of millet carrying the weight of life. There is an inseverable blood link between Chinese and millet in hundreds of generations.

感谢 / Acknowledgements

国家谷子改良中心
The National Millet Improvement Center

国家谷子高粱产业技术体系
The National Millet and Highlights Industrial Technology System

中央农业广播电视学校
The Central Agricultural Radio and Television School

中国农业科学院作物科学研究所
Institute of Crop Science, Chinese Academy of Agricultural Sciences

中国作物学会粟类作物专业委员会
Specialized Committee of Millet Crops of Chinese Crop Society

河北省农林科学院
Hebei Academy of Agriculture and Forestry Sciences

河北省农林科学院谷子研究所
Institute of Millet Crops, Hebei Academy of Agriculture and Forestry Sciences

河北省农林科学院对外合作处
Department of Foreign Affairs, Hebei Academy of Agriculture and Forestry Sciences

河北省杂粮研究实验室
Laboratory of Coarse Crops of Hebei Province

河北省老科学技术工作者协会
Hebei Association of Senior Scientists and Technicians

感谢 / Acknowledgements

河北省中医院
Hebei Hospital of Traditional Chinese Medicine

河北省饮食服务商会
Hebei Catering Service Chamber of Commerce

河北省军区第十三离职干部休养所
Hebei Military Area Command Thirteenth Demobilized Cadres Rest Home

贵州省农业科学院
Guizhou Academy of Agricultural Sciences

甘肃省农业科学院
Gansu Academy of Agricultural Sciences

张家口市农业科学院
Zhangjiakou Agricultural Science Research Institute，Hebei Province

安阳市农业科学院
Anyang Academy of Agricultural Sciences Henan Province

淄博市农业科学研究院
Zibo Agricultural Science Research Institute Shangdong Province

延安市农业科学研究所
Yan'an Agricultural Science Research Institute Gansu Province

赤峰市农牧科学研究院
Chifeng Agricultural Science Research Institute Inner Monglia Autonomous Region

感谢 / Acknowledgements

吉林省农业机械研究院信息中心
Jilin Agricultural Machinery Research Institute Information Center
石家庄市妇产医院
Shijiazhuang Obstetrics and Gynecology Hospital
武安市人民政府
The People's Government of Wu'an City
中共怀来县委宣传部
Huailai County Party Committee Publicity Department of the CPC
中共蔚县县委宣传部
Yu County Publicity Department of the CPC
中共泊头市委宣传部
Botou Municipal Publicity Department of the CPC
中共涿鹿县委宣传部
Zhuolu County Party Committee Publicity Department of the CPC
中共南和县委宣传部
Nanhe County Party Committee Publicity Department of the CPC
中共赞皇县委宣传部
Zanhuang County Party Committee Publicity Department of the CPC
中共武安市委宣传部
Wu'an Municipal Committee Publicity Department of the CPC

感谢 / Acknowledgements

中共黄平县委宣传部
Huangping County Party Committee Publicity Department of the CPC
中共敖汉旗委宣传部
Aohan Banner Committee Publicity Department of the CPC
浙江建德市农业农村局
Zhejiang Jiande Agriculture and Rural Affairs Bureau
浙江东阳市农业农村局
Zhejiang Dongyang Agricultural and Rural Affairs Bureau
陕西延安市安塞区农业农村局
Shaanxi Yan'an Agricultural and Rural Affairs Bureau
甘肃白银市会宁县科技局
Gansu Baiyin Huining Science and Technology Bureau
河北武安磁山文化遗址博物馆
Cishan Cultural Heritage Museum, Wu'an Hebei Province
甘肃会宁红军长征胜利纪念馆
Gansu Huining Red Army Long March Victory Memorial Hall

图书在版编目（CIP）数据

粟说：一粒小米的故事 = The story of a millet：
汉英对照 / 王慧军，张韶斌主编 . — 北京：中国大地
出版社，2020.11
　ISBN 978-7-5200-0620-0

　Ⅰ . ①粟… Ⅱ . ①王… ②张… Ⅲ . ①谷子—通俗读
物—汉、英 Ⅳ . ① S515-49

　中国版本图书馆 CIP 数据核字 (2020) 第 133936 号

SUSHUO —— YI LI XIAOMI DE GUSHI

责任编辑：孙　灿　王丽丽
责任校对：王洪强
出版发行：中国大地出版社
社址邮编：北京市海淀区学院路 31 号，100083
电　　话：010 –66554649（邮购部）；010–66554610（编辑部）
网　　址：www.chinalandpress.com
印　　刷：河北远涛彩色印刷有限公司
开　　本：787mm × 1092mm　1/16
印　　张：14.75
字　　数：280 千字
版　　次：2020 年 11 月北京第 1 版
印　　次：2020 年 11 月石家庄第 1 次印刷
书　　号：ISBN 978-7-5200-0620-0
定　　价：98.00 元